Celebrating

100 YEARS

OF

JELL-O® BRAND

Publications International, Ltd.

JELL-O, KRAFT, ANGEL FLAKE, BAKER'S, BREAKSTONE'S, CALUMET, COOL WHIP, FREE, COOL WHIP LITE, DREAM WHIP, GENERAL FOODS INTERNATIONAL COFFEES, JIGGLERS, KID PACK, LIGHT N' LIVELY, MAXWELL HOUSE, MINUTE, MIRACLE WHIP, PHILADELPHIA BRAND, SNACKTIVITIES, STIR 'N SNACK, COOKIEWICHES, COOL 'N EASY and STILL THE COOLEST are trademarks of Kraft Foods, Inc., Northfield, IL 60093.

BREYERS is a registered trademark owned and licensed by Unilever N.V.

Desserts & Snacks Division Promotion Manager: Jeany Mui
Kraft Creative Kitchens Division Manager: Debra-Ann Robinson
Kraft Creative Kitchens Consumer Foods Associate: Mary Lee-Brody
Contributing Writer: Hunter & Associates, Inc., New York, NY

Photography: Sacco Productions Limited, Chicago
Photographers: Marc A. Frisco, Mike McKenzie
Photo Stylist: Melissa J. Frisco
Food Stylists: Amy Andrews, Gail O'Donnell, Bonnie Rabert, Teri Rys-Maki
Assistant Food Stylists: Kim Hartman, Susie Skoog

Photography (front cover): Creative Services/Kraft Photography Studio
Photographer: Gerry Zanetti
Photographer's Assistant: Philip Heimes
Food Stylist: Leslie Medina-Scocca
Assistant Food Stylist: Erna Krueger
Prop Stylist: Sandy Handloser
Art Direction: Ander Communications, Inc., New York, NY

Pictured on the front cover *(left to right):* Refreshers *(page 52),* Double Layer Chocolate Pie *(page 126),* Luscious Lemon Poke Cake *(page 170),* Cranberry Fruit Mold *(page 160),* Miniature Cheesecakes *(page 64).*

Pictured on the back cover *(clockwise from top left):* Striped Delight *(page 94),* Layered Pear Cream Cheese Mold *(page 28),* Sand Cup and Dirt Cups *(page 62),* COOL 'N EASY® Pie *(page 110).*

 Nutrition Information: We've provided nutrition information for some of the recipes in this publication, as now more than ever, people are interested in nutrition and health. These recipes will help you keep an eye on eating right without giving up food favorites or sacrificing taste for good nutrition. Remember, eating can be both healthy and enjoyable.

Microwave Cooking: Microwave ovens vary in wattage. The microwave cooking times given in this publication are approximate. Use the cooking times as guidelines and check for doneness before adding more time. Consult manufacturer's instructions for suitable microwave-safe cooking dishes.

Preparation/Cooking Times: Preparation times are based on the approximate amount of time required to assemble the recipe before cooking, baking, chilling or serving. These times include preparation steps such as measuring, chopping and mixing. The fact that some preparation and cooking can be done simultaneously is taken into account. Preparation of optional ingredients and serving suggestions is not included.

Celebrating 100 YEARS OF JELL-O® BRAND

After 100 Years...
Still The Coolest™!

Looking back 100 years ago, Jell-O was little more than a brand name and an unfulfilled dream.

Today, if placed end to end, the 299 million packages of Jell-O gelatin dessert produced in a year would stretch more than three fifths of the way around the globe. And the Jell-O brand now includes extensive lines of pudding mixes, No Bakes, snacks and yogurts—fun products which meet the needs of families today.

How did this phenomenon come about? How has this wiggly, jiggly product adapted to changes in lifestyles and eating habits to remain a brand recognized by 99% of Americans and used regularly in 72% of our homes?

Actually, the Jell-O story began more than 150 years ago. In 1845, the industrialist, inventor and philanthropist Peter Cooper, of Tom Thumb engine and Cooper Union fame, obtained the first patent for a gelatin dessert.

Although he packaged his gelatin in neat little boxes with directions for use, Cooper did very little to make the product more convenient to use. Home cooks still relied on sheets of prepared gelatin. These sheets had to be clarified by boiling them with egg whites and shells and then dripped through a jelly bag before they could be turned into shimmering molds.

An Inauspicious Beginning

In 1897, Pearl B. Wait, a carpenter and cough medicine manufacturer from LeRoy, New York, a quiet town in the western part of the state, decided to enter the packaged food business. Looking for a product, he came up with a fruit-flavored version of Cooper's gelatin. It was christened Jell-O by his wife, May Davis Wait, and was available in strawberry, raspberry, orange and lemon flavors. For two years Pearl Wait tried to sell Jell-O door-to-door, but he lacked the capital and sales experience to market it properly.

In frustration, Wait sold the Jell-O business for $450 to his LeRoy neighbor, Orator Francis Woodward, an entrepreneur who had founded the Genesee Pure Food Company two years earlier and successfully marketed Grain-O roasted cereal beverage. Woodward's first-year sales of Jell-O gelatin were so poor that one day, after touring the plant and seeing cases of Jell-O piled high, he offered the business to his plant superintendent for $35, a new low for the fledgling product. The offer was refused.

With the turn of the century came a new lease on life. Helped along by Woodward's creative sales and sampling strategies, Jell-O began to catch on. In 1902, when Woodward launched his first advertising campaign in women's magazines, sales reached $250,000. His first three-inch ad, costing $336 to place in one magazine, featured smiling, fashionably coifed women in white aprons proclaiming Jell-O gelatin "America's Most Famous Dessert."

Woodward's well-groomed sales force, sent out initially in handsome horse-drawn carriages and subsequently in late-model automobiles, attended every possible local party, fair, church social and picnic, offering to supply each event with free Jell-O gelatin. The salesmen demonstrated how easy it was to make the dessert and were generous with free samples and fancy molds.

The JELL-O Girl Stars in Ads

The Jell-O Girl, the brand's first trademark, made her debut in 1903 as the star of Woodward's second advertising campaign. The daughter of Franklin King, an artist for Genesee's ad agency, Elizabeth King was shown playing in her nursery, not with toys but with Jell-O packages. For the next four years, photos of Elizabeth were featured in magazine ads for Jell-O gelatin, on store displays, and on spoons, molds and china dessert dishes used as premiums, making the point that "you can't be a kid without it."

The first Jell-O recipe booklet appeared in 1904, stating that Jell-O gelatin was approved by pure food commissioners and touting it as a pure, wholesome and appetizing food, endorsed by physicians. The booklet also informed readers that Jell-O gelatin had won gold medals at the St. Louis Exposition in 1904 and the Portland Exposition in 1905. By this time, chocolate and cherry had joined the other four flavors.

In 1906, sales soared to just under the $1,000,000 mark. Shortly thereafter, Grain-O was taken off the market so the company could concentrate on the Jell-O brand. When Orator Woodward passed away, his wife, Cora Talmadge Woodward, succeeded him as president of the company. Canadian production began that year in Bridgeburg, Ontario. Peach flavor joined the line in 1907.

Kewpie Dolls Sell JELL-O

In 1908, artist Rose O'Neill, who created the famous cheerful Kewpie dolls, modernized the Jell-O Girl, when one of her renderings appeared on the package design. Children continued to be featured in ads and recipe booklets. Also, O'Neill's Kewpies, which were a regular feature in *Good Housekeeping* magazine as well as Jell-O ads and booklets, delighted thousands of children.

In the first quarter of the century, an estimated quarter billion Jell-O recipe booklets were printed in several languages, including German, Spanish, Swedish and Yiddish, and distributed door-to-door. Messages emphasized ease of preparation, low cost, purity, perfection of flavor, beauty and variety. "The easy Jell-O way" was put forth for people who didn't have time to be housewives, a concept endorsed by Rose O'Neill, a working woman herself.

Packaging of the product was updated in 1914 with automatic equipment and a new seamless sealed wax paper bag that was more effective in keeping moisture out. Two years later, Ernest Woodward took over the presidency of the company from his mother.

In 1917, Jell-O recipe booklets commented on the wartime economy, reassuring homemakers that "while war prices prevail and nearly everything has gone up, Jell-O gelatin still sells for ten cents, and the people's favorite dessert continues to be enjoyed at the old low cost."

The Twenties Bring Major Changes

Recipes like Peach Champagne Sparkle, Jellied Manhattan Salad and Egg Slices en Gelée reflected the flamboyance of this era.

During the 1920's, three significant developments affected the Jell-O brand. In 1923, the Genesee Pure Food Company introduced D-Zerta, the first sugar-free gelatin dessert. In November of the same year, Genesee changed its name to the Jell-O Company in a move to protect its famous trademark. In 1925, the Postum Company acquired the Jell-O Company, forming the nucleus of what would become General Foods Corporation. The product Wait sold to Woodward in 1899 for $450 was now a business worth $67,000,000.

Jell-O advertising in the 1920's included some of the most beautiful food illustrations ever created by outstanding artists such as Guy Rowe (Giro), Linn Ball and Maxfield Parrish. Other ads by Norman Rockwell showed the ease of making Jell-O with appealing family scenes, such as a little girl unmolding a Jell-O treat for her doll and a grandmother making Jell-O with her grandchildren.

In 1929, the Jell-O Company acquired Genesee Pudding Powder, a company that made vanilla, lemon, butterscotch and chocolate pudding mixes for the institutional market. The chocolate flavor was marketed to consumers as Walter Baker Dessert. It became Jell-O Chocolate Pudding in 1936. Vanilla and butterscotch were added two years later. Jell-O pudding became available in 51 varieties and remained a top-selling prepared dessert.

Salad Days Lead to Lime

Gelled, or "congealed," salads became very popular around this time, with almost one third of the salad recipes in the average cookbook gelatin-based. This led to the introduction of lime flavored Jell-O in 1930, a flavor well-suited to salads, appetizers, relishes and entrées. The advent of the automatic refrigerator gave Jell-O a real boost, making it easier and twice as fast to create family favorites like Sunset Salad and Paradise Pudding and stylish geometrical molds reflecting the Art Deco age.

Jell-O production began in Los Angeles the next year, and the Canadian operation moved from Bridgeburg, Ontario, to Montreal, Quebec. The brand's involvement with children continued with the sponsorship of a Wizard of Oz radio program and a series of children's booklets by Frank L. Baum, author of the Wizard of Oz books.

The Benny Era

"Jell-O again" became a familiar greeting over the radio air waves as Jack Benny, Mary Livingston, Don Wilson

and the unforgettable J-E-L-L-O song brought Jell-O into millions of American homes every Sunday evening for ten years starting in 1934. Recipe booklets featured the brand of humor so typical of Jack and Mary.

At the end of the decade, production expanded to plants in Hoboken, New Jersey and Chicago, Illinois. The company continued to experiment with new products, bringing out unflavored gelatin in 1936 as well as a cola flavor for kids in 1942, which was discontinued in the following year.

JELL-O Goes to War

In 1942, the sugar wartime shortage forced the company to change its package weights. Jell-O pudding sponsored the Kate Smith Hour on radio and featured her in print advertising with patriotic themes

A sign of the times in 1944 was the publication of war-related recipe booklets. One called "Bright Spots for Wartime Meals—66 Ration-Wise Recipes" offered recipes using few or no ration point ingredients and ideas designed to stretch every bit of fruit, egg or cream. Because of the scarcity of shortening, one-crust pies became popular, with fillings made with Jell-O gelatin or pudding. As late as 1946, Jell-O ads were still apologizing for product shortages related to scarcity of sugar. Time-pressed consumers were also introduced to the "speed set" method of making Jell-O gelatin, using ice cubes for part of the cold water called for in the directions.

Later, Jell-O rice pudding was introduced in 1948 and 1949 along with three flavors of Jell-O tapioca pudding—vanilla, chocolate and orange-coconut. Recognizing the dual use of its pudding products, General Foods decided to rename and promote this line as puddings and pie fillings. Jell-O Instant Pudding was test marketed the next year.

Lighthearted in the Fifties

Jell-O grape gelatin made its debut in 1950, followed later in the decade by apple, black cherry, black raspberry, and six-ounce family-size packages for the popular red fruit flavors. No longer promoted as a food-stretcher, Jell-O took a light-hearted approach and positioned itself as a treat and festive dessert to be served with pride. Ads campaigned for National Trim-Your-Torso-with-Jell-O Week, National Use-Up-Your-Leftovers-in-a-Jell-O-Salad Week and National Jell-O-with-Fruit-to-Boot Week. One-crust gelatin and ice cream parfait pies became all the rage. Jell-O sales reached over 250 million packages a year.

Jell-O Instant Pudding went national in 1953 with chocolate, vanilla and butterscotch flavors. Shortly afterwards, coconut cream, lemon and strawberry were introduced to consumers. Advertised on network television, these products were promoted as "Busy Day Desserts," stressing that there is always enough time for real homemade desserts.

The Sensational Sixties

For Jell-O gelatin, the 1960's was a decade of expansion and experimentation with flavors. In this period, six flavors were discontinued, but eighteen new flavors were introduced.

Jell-O and fruit was the promotion of the decade with simple combinations in salads and desserts. The classic cookbook *The Joys of Jell-O* was published and has since gone through many printings and revisions with sales in the millions.

Puddings were expanding as well in the 1960's, with pineapple cream and caramel bringing the number of flavors in the instant pudding category to eight. Chocolate-mint, chocolate fudge, banana cream, real lime, pineapple cream, milk chocolate and French vanilla were added to the pudding and pie filling line. Lemon and orange tapioca pudding mixes rolled out nationally.

The first Jell-O No Bake Dessert, a real cheesecake that requires no baking and takes only 15 minutes to prepare, was launched in 1967. This dry packaged product includes crust, filling mix and topping. The convenience of making a spectacular dessert in a short time without baking made this product an immediate hit with working women.

Faster Is Better

With this new-found time pressure, "faster is better" became the Jell-O gelatin thrust of the 1970's. Consumers were offered preparation shortcuts using ice cubes, frozen fruit, ice cream, a blender or an ice bath. Make-ahead fruit and vegetable salads were promoted to complete the evening meal, leading to the creation of fruit salad flavors—cranberry orange, pineapple, mandarin orange and apple. Peach flavor reappeared.

As convenience became a higher priority for consumers, Jell-O Pudding Treats, puddings in single-serving size cans, were brought out in 1971.

In 1974, Bill Cosby became the spokesperson for Jell-O brand pudding. His vibrant, upbeat personality was perfect to project the idea that Jell-O is a fun food for kids. He began with the "Kids Love Pudding" campaign, and this synergistic relationship continues to this day. New flavors in 1976 were Americana rice pudding and pistachio instant pudding. Popular recipes were Pudding in a Cloud and in 1981, Watergate Salad (Pistachio and Pineapple Delight).

Blackberry flavor gelatin reappeared in 1981. That year also saw Jell-O marketed in recipe canisters and the introduction of Jell-O Brand Gelatin Pops. Two years later, Sugar Free Jell-O Gelatin appeared to fit with healthier contemporary family lifestyles. A second convenient Jell-O No Bake Dessert, Chocolate Silk Pie, was successfully launched in 1984.

Cosby Speaks for JELL-O Gelatin, Too

After 13 years promoting pudding, Bill Cosby was so successful in appealing to young moms and kids that he became the spokesperson for Jell-O gelatin as well. Sales, which had been lackluster, began to turn around as baby boomers started families and served foods they loved as kids to their own children.

Jell-O JIGGLERS® gelatin snacks were introduced in 1988, with the company's Consumer Response Center receiving 150 to 200 calls daily requesting the recipe for

7

this colorful fingerfood snack for kids. Jell-O Man made a brief appearance in ads and booklets. Sugar Free Jell-O gelatin snacks in cup form were introduced nationally.

Snacktivities® Cool for Kids

From Jigglers came the Snacktivities recipes and games promotion encouraging parents and kids to make fun recipes together using Jell-O gelatin and pudding—fanciful edibles like Dirt Cups, Aquarium Cups and Poke Cake. New watermelon and Berry Blue gelatin flavors appealed to youngsters, grape reappeared with the help of dinosaurs from Jurassic Park, and blackberry was reincarnated as Berry Black. Traditionally, blue has not been a big food color, but today's kids think it's cool. Launched in 1992, Berry Blue sold 21 million packages in its first year.

In 1995, cranberry, cranberry-raspberry and cranberry-strawberry entered the line, capitalizing on the growing popularity of cranberry flavor and color in everything from vodka to salad dressings. Other 1990's innovations include Jell-O Microwave Pudding and Pie Filling, Jell-O Free Pudding snacks made with skim milk and Jell-O Sugar Free Fat Free Instant Pudding & Pie Filling. The new Jell-O® Stir 'n Snack™ Chocolate and Vanilla Instant Pudding Mixes in canisters have the flexibility of making one serving at a time and are ready to eat in just five minutes. Seven luscious new Jell-O No Bake desserts made their debuts, each with crust, filling mix and topping, and some with appealing double layers.

Capitalizing on the healthfulness of low fat yogurts and kids' love of Jell-O, the brand now offers Jell-O® Yogurt Kid Pack® Low Fat Multipacks. These come in a variety of creamy fruit flavors, some containing Jigglers bits for extra fun and flavor.

In 1995, Jell-O Jigglers eggs were launched. They are formed by molds that produce three-dimensional jewel-like gelatin snacks in the size and shape of real eggs. More than 15,000 of these were handed out to children attending the annual Easter Egg Roll at the White House.

JELL-O in Space

Jell-O in space made news in June 1996. According to a Reuters dispatch, Shannon Lucid, the American astronaut on a 140-day mission in the Russian Mir space station, revealed that she kept track of time by allowing herself to wear pink socks and eat Jell-O on Sundays.

Tropical Blends—strawberry kiwi, peach passion fruit and island pineapple—are the latest Jell-O excitement, along with a delightful fizz-capturing recipe for Jell-O Refreshers, made by substituting seltzer, club soda or carbonated lemon-lime beverage for the cold water called for in the directions.

From Nostalgia Fans to Web Sites

Today Jell-O products are not only the largest selling prepared desserts, but the brand is one of the best known in the whole field of grocery products. Its history through the years has been one of adapting to contemporary consumer needs and desires, and it continues to do so. The brand is a popular and familiar icon. In addition to the gelatin restaurant and museum devoted to Jell-O, there are Jell-O fans and memorabilia collectors all over the country. Now there is even a Jell-O home page on the Kraft Foods, Inc. Web site at http://www.kraftfoods.com.

Over 100 varieties of snacks and desserts are sold under the Jell-O brand. In the United States, every eight seconds someone buys a package of Jell-O gelatin, the dessert from LeRoy, New York, that started it all 100 years ago. We invite you to page through this spectacular collection of Jell-O recipes for dozens of ideas sure to please one and all. Enjoy!

8

Tips and Techniques

All of the recipes appearing in this publication have been developed and tested by the food professionals in the JELL-O Test Kitchens to ensure your success in making them. We also share our JELL-O secrets with you. These foolproof tips, many with step-by-step photos, help you get perfect results every time. And the quick garnish ideas are sure to add pizzazz to your recipes, impressing family and friends alike.

GELATIN

Making JELL-O Brand Gelatin Dessert is easy. Just follow the package directions and the results will be a success.

The basic directions as written below are also on the package:

- Stir 1 cup boiling water into 1 package (4-serving size) gelatin at least 2 minutes until completely dissolved. Stir in 1 cup cold water. Refrigerate 4 hours or until firm. (For an 8-serving size package, use 2 cups boiling water and 2 cups cold water.)

- JELL-O Brand Sugar Free Low Calorie Gelatin Dessert is prepared in the same way. It can be used in many recipes that call for JELL-O Brand Gelatin Dessert.

Some Tips for Success

- To make a mixture that is clear and uniformly set, make sure the gelatin is completely dissolved in boiling water or other boiling liquid before adding the cold water.

- To double a recipe, simply double the amount of gelatin, liquid and other ingredients used except salt, vinegar and lemon juice. For these ingredients, use 1½ times the amount given in the recipe.

- To store prepared gelatin overnight or longer, cover it before refrigerating to prevent drying. Always store gelatin desserts and molds in the refrigerator.

- Generally, gelatin molds are best served right from the refrigerator. A gelatin mold containing fruit or vegetables can remain at room temperature up to 2 hours. Always keep a gelatin mold containing meat, mayonnaise, ice cream or other dairy products refrigerated until ready to serve. Also, do not let it sit at room temperature longer than 30 minutes. Store any leftover gelatin mold in the refrigerator.

How to Speed Up Refrigerating Time

- Choose the right container. Use a metal bowl or mold rather than glass, plastic or china. Metal chills more quickly and the gelatin will be firm in less time than in glass or plastic bowls.

- Use the speed set (ice cube) method. (Do not use this method if you are going to mold gelatin.) For a 4-serving size package, stir ¾ cup boiling water into gelatin in medium bowl at least 2 minutes until completely dissolved. Mix ½ cup cold water and ice cubes to make 1¼ cups. Add to gelatin, stirring until slightly thickened. Remove any remaining ice. Refrigerate 30 minutes for a soft set or 1 to 1½ hours until firm. (For an 8-serving size package, use 1½ cups boiling water. Mix 1 cup cold water and ice cubes to make 2½ cups.)

- Use the ice bath method. (This method will speed up the preparation of layered gelatin molds.) Prepare gelatin as directed on package. Place bowl of gelatin in a larger bowl of ice and water. Stir occasionally as mixture chills to ensure even thickening.

- Use the blender method. (This method can be used to make quick and easy layered gelatin desserts.) Place 1 package (4-serving size) gelatin and ¾ cup boiling liquid in blender container; cover. Blend on low speed about 30 seconds or until gelatin is completely dissolved. Mix ½ cup cold water and ice cubes to make 1¼ cups. Add to gelatin, stirring until partially melted; cover. Blend on low speed 30 seconds. Pour into dessert dishes or bowl. Refrigerate at least 30 minutes or until set. The mixture is self-layering and sets with a frothy layer on top and a clear layer on bottom. (Use this method for 4-serving size package only. The volume of liquid required for an 8-serving size package is too large for most blenders.)

Gelatin Refrigerating Time Chart

In all recipes, for best results, the gelatin needs to be refrigerated to the proper consistency. Use this chart as a guideline to determine the desired consistency and the approximate refrigerating time.

When a recipe says:	It means gelatin should:	Refrigerating Time		Gelatin Uses
		Regular set	Speed set*	
"Refrigerate until syrupy"	Be consistency of thick syrup	1 hour	3 minutes	Glaze for pies, fruit
"Refrigerate until slightly thickened"	Be consistency of unbeaten egg whites	1¼ hours	5 to 6 minutes	Adding creamy ingredients such as whipped topping, or when mixture will be beaten
"Refrigerate until thickened"	Be thick enough so that a spoon drawn through it leaves a definite impression	1½ hours	7 to 8 minutes	Adding solid ingredients such as fruits or vegetables
"Refrigerate until set but not firm"	Stick to finger when touched and mound or move to the side when bowl or mold is tilted	2 hours	30 minutes	Layering gelatin mixtures
"Refrigerate until firm"	Not stick to finger when touched and not mound or move when mold is tilted	Individual molds: at least 3 hours 2- to 6-cup mold: at least 4 hours 8- to 12-cup mold: at least 5 hours or overnight		Unmolding and serving

*Speed set (ice cube) method is not recommended for molding.

Gelatin Consistencies

Syrupy gelatin should be consistency of thick syrup.

Slightly thickened gelatin should be consistency of unbeaten egg whites.

Thickened gelatin should be thick enough so that a spoon drawn through it leaves a definite impression.

Set but not firm gelatin should stick to finger when touched and mound or move to the side when bowl or mold is tilted.

Firm gelatin should not stick to finger when touched and not mound or move when mold is tilted.

The Secret to Molding Gelatin

The Mold

- Use metal molds, traditional decorative molds and other metal forms, or plastic molds. You can use square or round cake pans, fluted or plain tube pans, loaf pans, or metal mixing bowls (nested sets give you a variety of sizes). You can also use metal fruit or juice cans. (To unmold, dip can in warm water, then puncture bottom of can and unmold.)

- To determine the volume of the mold, measure first with water. Most recipes give an indication of the size of the mold needed. For clear gelatin, you need a 2-cup mold for a 4-serving size package and a 4-cup mold for an 8-serving size package.

- If mold holds less than the size called for, pour the extra gelatin into a separate dish. Refrigerate and serve it at another time. Do not use a mold that is too large, since it would be difficult to unmold.

- For easier unmolding, spray mold with no stick cooking spray before filling mold.

The Preparation

- To prepare gelatin for molding, use less water than the amount called for on the package. For a 4-serving size package, decrease cold water to ¾ cup. For an 8-serving size package, decrease cold water to 1½ cups. (This adjustment has already been made in the recipes in this book.) The firmer consistency will result in a less fragile mold. It also makes unmolding much simpler.

- To prevent spilling, place mold on tray in refrigerator before pouring in gelatin.

- To arrange fruits or vegetables in the mold, refrigerate gelatin until thickened. (If gelatin is not thick enough, fruits or vegetables may sink or float.) Pour gelatin into mold to about ¼-inch depth. Reserve remaining gelatin at room temperature. Arrange fruits or vegetables in decorative pattern on gelatin. Refrigerate mold until gelatin is set but not firm. Spoon reserved gelatin over pattern in mold. Refrigerate until firm, then unmold.

The Unmolding

- First, allow gelatin to set until firm by refrigerating several hours or overnight. Also chill serving plate or individual plates on which mold is to be served by storing in refrigerator.

- Make certain that gelatin is completely firm. It should not feel sticky on top and should not mound or move to the side if mold is tilted.

- Moisten tips of fingers and gently pull gelatin from around edge of mold. Or, use a small metal spatula or pointed knife dipped in warm water to loosen top edge.

- Dip mold in warm, not hot, water just to the rim for about 15 seconds. Lift from water, hold upright and shake to loosen gelatin. Or, gently pull gelatin from edge of mold.

- Moisten chilled serving plate with water. (This allows gelatin to be moved after unmolding.) Place moistened serving plate on top of mold. Invert mold and plate; holding mold and plate together, shake slightly to loosen. Gently remove mold. If gelatin does not release easily, dip mold in warm water again for a few seconds. Center gelatin on serving plate.

Unmolding

1. Before unmolding, gently pull gelatin from around edge of mold with moist fingertips.

2. Dip mold in warm water, just to the rim, for about 15 seconds.

3. Lift mold from water, hold upright and shake to loosen gelatin.

4. Place moistened serving plate on top of mold.

5. Invert mold and plate; shake to loosen gelatin.

6. Remove mold and center gelatin on plate.

13

Simple Additions

Fruits and Vegetables

- Refrigerate gelatin until thickened. For a 4-serving size package, add ¾ to 1½ cups sliced or chopped fruit or vegetables. (For an 8-serving size package, add 1½ to 3 cups.) Do not use fresh or frozen pineapple, kiwi, gingerroot, papaya, figs or guava. An enzyme in these fruits will prevent the gelatin from setting. However, if cooked or canned, these fruits may be used. Drain canned or fresh fruits well before adding to the gelatin. The fruit juice or syrup can be used to replace part of the cold water used in preparing the gelatin.

- Some favorite fresh fruits include apples, bananas, peaches, oranges, grapefruit, melons, grapes, pears, strawberries, blueberries and raspberries. Canned fruits include peaches, pineapple, pears, apricots, mandarin oranges, cherries and fruit cocktail. Dried fruits, such as raisins, currants, figs, dates, apricots or prunes, can be added to gelatin. Nuts, such as coconut, walnuts, pecans and almonds, can also be used.

- Gelatin salads can include fresh vegetables, such as carrots, celery, peppers, onions, cucumbers, tomatoes or summer squash. Serve them on crisp salad greens.

Carbonated Beverages

Substitute cold carbonated beverages, such as seltzer, club soda, fruit-flavored seltzer, ginger ale or a lemon-lime carbonated beverage, for part or all of the cold water. (Do not use tonic water.)

Fruit Juice or Iced Tea

Use fruit juices, such as orange, apple, cranberry, canned pineapple or white grape juice, for part of the cold water. Nectars, such as apricot, peach and mango, or juice blends and drinks can also be substituted. Or, use iced tea, plain or flavored, for part of the cold water.

Flavored Extracts

Add just a touch of flavoring extracts, such as vanilla, almond, peppermint or rum, for additional flavor.

Citrus Fruits

Adding grated orange, lemon or lime peel and lemon or lime juice will add zing to your gelatin. Add 1 teaspoon grated peel and/or 1 tablespoon juice to a 4-serving size package of gelatin. For an 8-serving size package, use 1½ teaspoons grated peel and 1½ tablespoons juice.

Ways to Add Extra Flair to Gelatin

Flake or Cube It

Prepare gelatin as directed on package, decreasing cold water to ¾ cup for a 4-serving size package. (For an 8-serving size package, decrease cold water to 1½ cups.) Pour into a shallow pan. Refrigerate about 3 hours or until firm.

- To flake, break gelatin into small flakes with fork or force through a large mesh strainer. Pile flakes of gelatin lightly into dessert dishes. Serve with fruit or whipped topping, if desired.

- To cube, cut gelatin into small cubes, using a sharp knife that has been dipped in warm water. Dip pan quickly in warm water. Remove cubes with a serving spoon or spatula. Serve in dessert dishes with fruit or whipped topping, if desired.

Layer It

- Layer different flavors of gelatin for a clear multi-colored mold.

- For a clear and creamy layered mold, first layer clear gelatin, then top with a layer of gelatin mixed with either whipped topping, yogurt, ice cream or cream cheese. Refrigerate each layer only until set but not firm before adding the next layer. If the lower layer is too firm, the layers will not adhere to each other and the layers may slip apart when unmolded. The gelatin should stick to finger when touched and move gently from side to side when the mold or bowl is tilted. Except for the first layer, the gelatin mixtures should be cool and slightly thickened before pouring into the mold. A warm mixture could soften the layer beneath it and cause the mixtures to run together.

PUDDING

The recipes in this book use both JELL-O Cook & Serve Pudding & Pie Filling, which requires cooking, and JELL-O Instant Pudding & Pie Filling, which is not cooked. These products are not interchangeable in recipes. Be sure to use the product called for in the recipe.

JELL-O Instant Pudding & Pie Filling is also available Fat Free. Both the Instant and the Cook & Serve Pudding & Pie Fillings are also available as Sugar Free Fat Free.

See individual packages for basic directions for preparing the products as either a pudding or a pie filling.

Some Tips for Success

For JELL-O Instant Pudding & Pie Filling

- Always use cold milk. Beat pudding mix slowly, not vigorously.

- For best results, use 2% lowfat milk or whole milk. Skim, 1% lowfat, reconstituted nonfat dry milk or lactose-reduced milk can also be used. For Fat Free or Sugar Free Fat Free Pudding & Pie Filling, use cold skim milk.

- Always store prepared pudding desserts, pies and snacks in the refrigerator.

For JELL-O Cook & Serve Pudding & Pie Filling

- It's best to cook the pudding in a heavy saucepan to ensure even heating. Stir pudding mixture constantly as it cooks. Make sure it comes to full boil. The mixture will be thin, but will thicken as it cools.

- For a creamier pudding, place a piece of plastic wrap on the surface of pudding while cooling. Stir before serving.

- To cool pudding quickly, place saucepan of hot pudding in larger pan of ice water; stir frequently until mixture is cooled. Do not use this method for pie filling.

Simple Additions

- Stir mix-ins such as chopped candy bar, chopped cookies, candy-coated milk chocolate candies, butterscotch or peanut butter chips, BAKER'S Semi-Sweet Real Chocolate Chips, miniature marshmallows, nuts or toasted BAKER'S ANGEL FLAKE Coconut into prepared pudding just before serving.

- Stir fruit such as chopped banana or strawberries, raspberries, blueberries, mandarin orange segments or drained canned fruit cocktail into prepared pudding just before serving.

- For spiced pudding, stir ½ teaspoon ground cinnamon into a 4-serving size package of pudding mix before adding cold milk.

NO BAKE CHEESECAKES and DESSERTS

Some Tips for Success

- The cheesecake can also be prepared in an 8- or 9-inch square pan or 12 foil- or paper-lined muffin cups.

- Two packages of the cheesecake can be prepared in a 13×9-inch pan or a 9×3-inch springform pan.

- To serve, dip the pie plate just to the rim in hot water for 30 seconds before cutting.

- To freeze, cover the cheesecake. Freeze up to 2 weeks. Thaw in refrigerator 3 hours before serving.

- For easy cleanup, line the 8- or 9-inch square pan with foil before preparing the No Bake Dessert.

- The No Bake Desserts can also be served frozen. Freeze 4 hours or until firm. Remove from freezer and serve immediately.

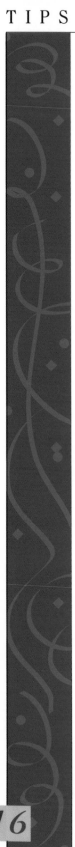

EASY GARNISHING TIPS

It's those finishing touches that make the professional's desserts so special. Here are their secrets.

Whipped Topping Dollops

1. Swirl spoon, held upright, through thawed COOL WHIP Whipped Topping, creating rippled surface on the topping.

2. Dip spoon into rippled topping to scoop up heaping spoonful of topping, maintaining rippled surface.

3. Gently touch spoon onto surface of dessert and release topping gradually onto surface, pulling spoon up into a crowning tip.

Whipped Topping Piping

1. Insert decorating tip in pastry bag. Fill with thawed COOL WHIP Whipped Topping. Fold down top of pastry bag.

2. Holding bag firmly with one hand, squeeze topping down into tip. Guide tip around surface to be decorated. Double back topping at intervals for decorative wave effect.

Fruit Fans

Cut whole strawberry into thin slices, cutting from pointed end to, but not through, stem end. Gently fan out slices from stem.

Citrus Twists

Cut orange into thin slices. Cut a slit through each slice from center to edge. Twist slices from slits in opposite directions to form twists.

Tinted Coconut

Dilute a few drops of food coloring with ½ teaspoon water; add to 1 cup coconut in plastic bag. Close bag; shake until coconut is evenly tinted. Repeat with more food coloring and water for darker shade.

Toasted Coconut or Nuts

Heat oven to 350°F. Spread 1 cup coconut or nuts in an even layer in shallow baking pan. Toast 7 to 9 minutes for coconut or 8 to 10 minutes for nuts, until lightly browned. Stir the coconut or nuts frequently so that they brown evenly. Or, toast in the microwave in microwavable pie plate on HIGH about 5 minutes, stirring several times.

Easy Chocolate Garnishes

Use BAKER'S Semi-Sweet, Bittersweet, Premium White or GERMAN'S Sweet Baking Chocolate and follow the melting tips below.

Easy Microwave Melting

For Semi-Sweet, Bittersweet or Premium White Chocolate: Heat 1 square chocolate, unwrapped, in microwavable bowl on HIGH 1 to 2 minutes, stirring halfway through heating time. The square will retain some of its original shape. Remove from oven. Stir until completely melted. Add 10 seconds for each additional square of chocolate.

For GERMAN'S Sweet Chocolate: Heat 1 bar chocolate, unwrapped and broken in half, in microwavable bowl on HIGH 1½ to 2 minutes, stirring halfway through heating time. The bar will retain some of its original shape. Remove from oven. Stir until completely melted.

Top of Stove Melting

Place chocolate in heavy saucepan on very low heat; stir constantly until just melted.

Chocolate Drizzle

1. Place 1 square of chocolate in heavy-duty zipper-style plastic bag. Close tightly. Microwave on HIGH 30 seconds. Squeeze bag gently to melt chocolate. Roll up bag to push chocolate into corner. Cut off tiny piece of corner ($\frac{1}{8}$ inch).

2. Gently squeeze bag to drizzle chocolate over cookies, fruit, pie or cake.

Chocolate Dipper Garnish

1. Dip fruit, cookies, pretzels, dried apricots, large marshmallows and candy canes into melted chocolate; let excess chocolate drip off.

2. Arrange on wax paper-lined cookie sheet. Let stand at room temperature 30 minutes or refrigerate until chocolate is firm.

Chocolate Curls

1. Spread 4 squares melted chocolate with spatula into very thin layer on cookie sheet. Refrigerate about 10 minutes or until firm but still pliable.

2. To make curls, push metal spatula firmly along cookie sheet, under chocolate, so that chocolate curls as it is pushed. (If chocolate is too firm to curl, let stand a few minutes at room temperature. If chocolate is too soft to curl, refrigerate it again until firm.)

3. Carefully pick up each chocolate curl by inserting toothpick in center. Lift onto wax paper-lined cookie sheet. Refrigerate about 15 minutes or until firm. Arrange on dessert.

Shaved Chocolate

Pull vegetable peeler across surface of chocolate square, using short, quick strokes. Sprinkle the shaved chocolate on desserts or beverages.

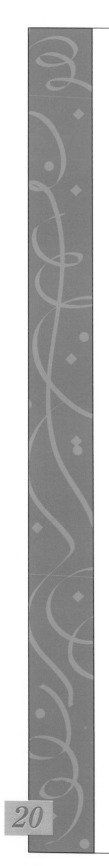

Shimmering Molds

Four out of six recipes in the very first JELL-O recipe folder issued in 1902 called for the gelatin mixtures to be poured into "moulds" and set in a cool place until firm. Molded gelatin dishes, with their decorative shapes and garnishes, appeared at many a meal for family and guests, as salads, relishes and gorgeous desserts—each one served with great pride.

In the 1920's, beautiful JELL-O ads by famous illustrators depicted the shimmery transparency of jewel-like molds, truly the stars of any dining situation. Here are molds—some clear, some creamy, some layered—for you to try. You'll have fun making them and will be thrilled with the results!

21

Top to bottom: Cranberry Cream Cheese Mold (page 36), Sunset Fruit Salad (page 24), White Sangria Splash (page 37), Cucumber Sour Cream Mold (page 25)

Gazpacho Salad

1903

This jazzed-up variation on tomato aspic adopts the flavor and texture of the famous Spanish cold soup.

Enjoy the taste of Spain with this fat free tangy salad.

    1 cup diced tomato
  ½ cup diced peeled cucumber
  ¼ cup diced green pepper
    2 tablespoons diced red pepper
    2 tablespoons thinly sliced green onion
    2 tablespoons vinegar
  ¼ teaspoon pepper
  ⅛ teaspoon garlic powder (optional)
1½ cups tomato juice
    1 package (4-serving size) JELL-O Brand Lemon Flavor Sugar Free Low Calorie Gelatin Dessert or JELL-O Brand Lemon Flavor Gelatin Dessert
Crackers (optional)

MIX vegetables, vinegar, pepper and garlic powder in medium bowl; set aside. Bring tomato juice to boil in small saucepan. Stir into gelatin in large bowl at least 2 minutes until completely dissolved. Refrigerate about 1¼ hours or until slightly thickened (consistency of unbeaten egg whites).

STIR in vegetable mixture. Pour into 4-cup mold.

REFRIGERATE 3 hours or until firm. Unmold. Serve with crackers if desired. Garnish as desired.

Makes 6 servings

 *Nutrition Information Per Serving (using JELL-O Brand Lemon Flavor Sugar Free Low Calorie Gelatin Dessert and omitting crackers and garnish):* 30 calories, 0g fat, 0mg cholesterol, 260mg sodium, 5g carbohydrate, less than 1g dietary fiber, 4g sugars, 2g protein, 15% daily value vitamin A, 50% daily value vitamin C

Preparation Time: 20 minutes
Refrigerating Time: 4¼ hours

Gazpacho Salad

Sunset Fruit Salad

This spectacular fat free salad reflects the colors of the setting sun.

2 cups boiling water
1 package (4-serving size) JELL-O Brand Cranberry Flavor Sugar Free Low Calorie Gelatin Dessert or JELL-O Brand Cranberry Flavor Gelatin Dessert, or any red flavor
½ cup cold water
1 can (8 ounces) sliced peaches in juice, drained, chopped
1 package (4-serving size) JELL-O Brand Orange Flavor Sugar Free Low Calorie Gelatin Dessert or JELL-O Brand Orange Flavor Gelatin Dessert
1 can (8 ounces) crushed pineapple in juice, undrained

STIR 1 cup of the boiling water into cranberry gelatin in medium bowl at least 2 minutes until completely dissolved. Stir in cold water. Refrigerate about 45 minutes or until slightly thickened (consistency of unbeaten egg whites). Stir in peaches. Spoon into 5-cup mold. Refrigerate about 15 minutes or until set but not firm (gelatin should stick to finger when touched and should mound).

MEANWHILE, stir remaining 1 cup boiling water into orange gelatin in medium bowl at least 2 minutes until completely dissolved. Stir in pineapple with juice. Pour over gelatin layer in mold.

REFRIGERATE 4 hours or until firm. Unmold. Garnish as desired.

Makes 10 servings

 Nutrition Information Per Serving (using JELL-O Brand Cranberry and Orange Flavors Sugar Free Low Calorie Gelatin Dessert and omitting garnish): *30 calories, 0g fat, 0mg cholesterol, 60mg sodium, 6g carbohydrate, 0g dietary fiber, 7g sugars, 1g protein*

Preparation Time: 20 minutes
Refrigerating Time: 5 hours

Cucumber Sour Cream Mold

Complement poached salmon or shrimp with this refreshingly cool molded salad.

1½ **cups boiling water**
 1 **package (8-serving size) or 2 packages (4-serving size)**
   JELL-O Brand Lime Flavor Gelatin Dessert
 ¼ **teaspoon salt**
1½ **cups cold water**
 1 **tablespoon lemon juice**
 ½ **cup MIRACLE WHIP Salad Dressing**
 ½ **cup BREAKSTONE'S Sour Cream**
1½ **cups chopped seeded, peeled cucumber**
 2 **tablespoons minced onion**
 1 **teaspoon dill weed**

Molded salads are an elegant yet practical solution for dinner parties. Prepare them hours ahead of serving time.

STIR boiling water into gelatin and salt in large bowl at least 2 minutes until completely dissolved. Stir in cold water and lemon juice. Refrigerate about 1¼ hours or until slightly thickened (consistency of unbeaten egg whites).

MIX salad dressing and sour cream in small bowl until well blended. Stir into thickened gelatin. Refrigerate about 15 minutes or until thickened (spoon drawn through leaves definite impression). Stir in cucumbers, onion and dill weed. Pour into 5-cup mold.

REFRIGERATE 4 hours or until firm. Unmold. Garnish as desired.

Makes 10 servings

Preparation Time: 15 minutes
Refrigerating Time: 5½ hours

Mimosa Mold

It only takes a short time to prepare pretty gelatin molds, yet guests are so impressed with them.

1½ cups boiling water
1 package (8-serving size) or 2 packages (4-serving size)
    JELL-O Brand Sparkling White Grape or Lemon Flavor Gelatin Dessert
2 cups cold seltzer or club soda
1 can (11 ounces) mandarin orange segments, drained
1 cup sliced strawberries

STIR boiling water into gelatin in large bowl at least 2 minutes until completely dissolved. Stir in cold seltzer. Refrigerate 1½ hours or until thickened (spoon drawn through leaves definite impression). Stir in oranges and strawberries. Pour into 6-cup mold.

REFRIGERATE 4 hours or until firm. Unmold. Garnish as desired.

Makes 12 servings

Preparation Time: 15 minutes
Refrigerating Time: 5½ hours

Ginger Pineapple Mold

Don't try to use fresh pineapple or fresh ginger in this recipe because the enzymes they contain will prevent the gelatin from setting.

Catch the bubbles in this tangy salad.

1 can (20 ounces) crushed pineapple in juice, undrained
1½ cups boiling water
1 package (8-serving size) or 2 packages (4-serving size) JELL-O Brand Lime
    Flavor Gelatin Dessert
1 cup cold ginger ale or water
¼ teaspoon ground ginger

DRAIN pineapple, reserving juice. Stir boiling water into gelatin in large bowl at least 2 minutes until completely dissolved. Stir in reserved juice, ginger ale and ginger. Refrigerate about 1¼ hours or until slightly thickened (consistency of unbeaten egg whites).

STIR in pineapple. Pour into 5-cup mold.

REFRIGERATE 4 hours or until firm. Unmold.

Makes 10 servings

Preparation Time: 20 minutes
Refrigerating Time: 5¼ hours

Mimosa Mold

Layered Pear Cream Cheese Mold

Guests will enjoy this beautiful emerald-topped mold flavored with a hint of ginger.

Carbonated beverages add pizzazz to molded gelatin salads. Club soda, fruit-flavored sparkling water, ginger ale or lemon-lime flavored drinks can be substituted for all or part of the cold water.

1 can (16 ounces) pear halves, undrained
1 package (8-serving size) or 2 packages (4-serving size) JELL-O Brand Lime Flavor Gelatin Dessert
1½ cups cold ginger ale or water
2 tablespoons lemon juice
1 package (8 ounces) PHILADELPHIA BRAND Cream Cheese, softened
¼ cup chopped pecans

DRAIN pears, reserving liquid. Dice pears; set aside. Add water to liquid to make 1½ cups; bring to boil in small saucepan.

STIR boiling liquid into gelatin in large bowl at least 2 minutes until completely dissolved. Stir in cold ginger ale and lemon juice. Reserve 2½ cups gelatin at room temperature. Pour remaining gelatin into 5-cup mold. Refrigerate about 30 minutes or until thickened (spoon drawn through leaves definite impression). Arrange about ½ cup of the diced pears in thickened gelatin in mold.

STIR reserved 2½ cups gelatin gradually into cream cheese in large bowl with wire whisk until smooth. Refrigerate about 30 minutes or until slightly thickened (consistency of unbeaten egg whites). Stir in remaining diced pears and pecans. Spoon over gelatin layer in mold.

REFRIGERATE 4 hours or until firm. Unmold. Garnish as desired.

Makes 10 servings

Preparation Time: 30 minutes
Refrigerating Time: 5 hours

Layered Pear Cream Cheese Mold

Molded Seafood Mousse

Gelatin molds can be as simple or as elaborate as you wish to make them, but they are always impressive. It's fun to use your imagination when garnishing them with fruit or fresh vegetables.

When prepared in a fish-shaped mold, this mousse makes an impressive appetizer for a gala occasion.

- ¾ **cup boiling water**
- 1 **package (4-serving size) JELL-O Brand Lemon Flavor Gelatin Dessert**
- ¼ **teaspoon salt**
- 1 **cup BREAKSTONE'S Sour Cream**
- ½ **cup KRAFT Mayo: Real Mayonnaise or MIRACLE WHIP Salad Dressing**
- 2 **tablespoons horseradish**
- 2 **tablespoons lemon juice**
- 2 **tablespoons grated onion**
- 2 **cups seafood***
- 1½ **teaspoons dill weed**

STIR boiling water into gelatin and salt in large bowl at least 2 minutes until completely dissolved. Stir in sour cream, mayonnaise, horseradish, lemon juice and onion. Refrigerate about 1½ hours or until thickened (spoon drawn through leaves definite impression). Stir in seafood and dill weed. Spoon into 4-cup mold.

REFRIGERATE 3 hours or until firm. Unmold. Serve as an appetizer with crackers and raw vegetables.
Makes 12 servings

Suggested Seafood:
- 1 **can (15 or 16 ounces) red salmon, drained and flaked**
- 2 **cans (6 ounces each) crabmeat, drained and flaked**
- 2 **cups chopped cooked shrimp**
- 2 **cups chopped imitation crabmeat**

Preparation Time: 20 minutes
Refrigerating Time: 4½ hours

Creamy Fruited Lime Salad

Perfect for summer entertaining, this refreshing pineapple cream cheese mold hits the spot.

1½ **cups boiling water**
1 **package (8-serving size) or 2 packages (4-serving size) JELL-O Brand Lime Flavor Gelatin Dessert**
1 **can (8 ounces) crushed pineapple in juice, undrained**
1 **cup LIGHT N' LIVELY 1% Lowfat Cottage Cheese with Calcium**
1 **package (8 ounces) PHILADELPHIA BRAND Cream Cheese, softened**
1 **cup thawed COOL WHIP Whipped Topping**
½ **cup chopped walnuts**
¼ **cup chopped maraschino cherries**
Salad greens (optional)

STIR boiling water into gelatin in large bowl at least 2 minutes until completely dissolved. Stir in pineapple with juice. Refrigerate about 1¼ hours or until slightly thickened (consistency of unbeaten egg whites).

STIR cottage cheese into cream cheese in separate bowl until well blended. Gently stir in whipped topping until smooth. Beat into slightly thickened gelatin with wire whisk until well blended. Stir in walnuts and cherries. Pour into 6-cup mold.

REFRIGERATE 4 hours or until firm. Unmold. Serve on salad greens, if desired.

Makes 12 servings

Preparation Time: 15 minutes
Refrigerating Time: 5¼ hours

Gelatin molds, or "moulds" as it was spelled at the turn of the century, were a favorite "fancy" dessert. One early recipe for a molded Shredded Wheat JELL-O Apple Sandwich advised the reader, "Your tinner can make the mould for you" and went on to give the dimensions.

JELL-O® Fun Facts

Salt Lake City, Utah, ranks as the number one city in per capita consumption of JELL-O. The favorite flavor is lime. In fact, JELL-O is liked so much in Utah that there is a campaign to make it the official state food.

Vegetable Trio Mold

One of the joys of using JELL-O gelatin is the marvelous effect achieved by layering different flavors or different types of gelatin mixtures. Each layer should be chilled until just set, but not firm, before the next layer is added.

1907

A stunning use for fresh zucchini. The carrots and onions add flavor and crunch.

> 2 cups boiling water
> 1 package (8-serving size) or 2 packages (4-serving size) JELL-O Brand Lemon Flavor Gelatin Dessert
> ½ teaspoon salt
> 1½ cups cold water
> 3 tablespoons vinegar
> 1¼ cups grated carrots
> ½ cup KRAFT Mayo: Real Mayonnaise or MIRACLE WHIP Salad Dressing
> 1 cup shredded zucchini
> ¼ cup sliced green onions

STIR boiling water into gelatin and salt in large bowl at least 2 minutes until completely dissolved. Stir in cold water and vinegar. Reserve 2¾ cups gelatin at room temperature. Refrigerate remaining gelatin about 1 hour or until thickened (spoon drawn through leaves definite impression).

STIR carrots into thickened gelatin. Spoon into 5-cup mold. Refrigerate about 15 minutes or until set but not firm (gelatin should stick to finger when touched and should mound).

STIR 1 cup of the reserved gelatin into mayonnaise in medium bowl with wire whisk until smooth. Spoon over gelatin layer in mold. Refrigerate about 30 minutes or until set but not firm (gelatin should stick to finger when touched and should mound). Stir zucchini and green onions into remaining reserved gelatin. Spoon over gelatin layer in mold.

REFRIGERATE 3 hours or until firm. Unmold. Garnish as desired.   *Makes 10 servings*

Preparation Time: 30 minutes
Refrigerating Time: 4¾ hours

Vegetable Trio Mold

Sparkling Berry Salad

Capture the freshness of spring with this fat free berry-filled mold.

Fruit should be added to gelatin that has been chilled until it thickens, but is not yet set. This way, the fruit remains suspended in the gelatin.

2 cups boiling diet cranberry juice cocktail
1 package (8-serving size) or 2 packages (4-serving size) JELL-O Brand Sugar Free Low Calorie Gelatin Dessert or JELL-O Brand Gelatin Dessert, any red flavor
1½ cups cold seltzer or club soda
¼ cup creme de cassis liqueur (optional)
1 teaspoon lemon juice
3 cups assorted berries (blueberries, raspberries and sliced strawberries), divided

STIR boiling cranberry juice into gelatin in large bowl at least 2 minutes until completely dissolved. Stir in cold seltzer, liqueur and lemon juice. Refrigerate about 1½ hours or until slightly thickened (consistency of unbeaten egg whites).

STIR in 2 cups of the berries. Spoon into 5-cup mold.

REFRIGERATE 4 hours or until firm. Unmold. Top with remaining 1 cup berries.

Makes 8 servings

 Nutrition Information Per Serving (using JELL-O Brand Sugar Free Low Calorie Gelatin Dessert, liqueur and 1 cup each blueberries, raspberries and strawberries): *70 calories, 0g fat, 0mg cholesterol, 95mg sodium, 12g carbohydrate, 2g dietary fiber, 10g sugars, 2g protein, 50% daily value vitamin C*

Preparation Time: 15 minutes
Refrigerating Time: 5½ hours

Sparkling Berry Salad

Cranberry Cream Cheese Mold

Piquant cranberry flavor is one of the hits of the 1990's. Now you no longer have to save it just for the Thanksgiving holiday.

Add sparkle to your festive buffet with this dramatic double-layer fruit mold.

1½ **cups boiling water**
  1 **package (8-serving size) or 2 packages (4-serving size) JELL-O Brand Cranberry Flavor Gelatin Dessert, or any red flavor**
1½ **cups cold water**
  ½ **teaspoon ground cinnamon**
  1 **medium apple, chopped**
  1 **cup whole berry cranberry sauce**
  1 **package (8 ounces) PHILADELPHIA BRAND Cream Cheese, softened**

STIR boiling water into gelatin in large bowl at least 2 minutes until completely dissolved. Stir in cold water and cinnamon. Reserve 1 cup gelatin at room temperature. Refrigerate remaining gelatin about 1½ hours or until thickened (spoon drawn through leaves definite impression).

STIR apple and cranberry sauce into thickened gelatin. Spoon into 6-cup mold. Refrigerate about 30 minutes or until set but not firm (gelatin should stick to finger when touched and should mound).

STIR reserved 1 cup gelatin gradually into cream cheese in medium bowl with wire whisk until smooth. Pour over gelatin layer in mold.

REFRIGERATE 4 hours or until firm. Unmold. Garnish as desired.

Makes 12 servings

Note: *To prepare without cream cheese layer, omit cream cheese. Refrigerate all of the gelatin about 1½ hours or until thickened. Stir in apple and cranberry sauce. Pour into mold. Refrigerate.*

Preparation Time: 20 minutes
Refrigerating Time: 6 hours

White Sangria Splash

Wine adds the right touch to this fruity dessert.

1 cup dry white wine
1 package (8-serving size) or 2 packages (4-serving size) JELL-O Brand Lemon
    Flavor Sugar Free Low Calorie Gelatin Dessert or JELL-O Brand
    Lemon Flavor Gelatin Dessert
3 cups cold seltzer or club soda
1 tablespoon lime juice
1 tablespoon orange juice or orange liqueur
3 cups seedless grapes, divided
1 cup sliced strawberries
1 cup whole small strawberries

BRING wine to boil in small saucepan. Stir boiling wine into gelatin in medium bowl at least 2 minutes until completely dissolved. Stir in cold seltzer and lime and orange juices. Place bowl of gelatin in larger bowl of ice and water. Let stand about 10 minutes or until thickened (spoon drawn through leaves definite impression), stirring occasionally.

STIR in 1 cup of the grapes and the sliced strawberries. Pour into 6-cup mold.

REFRIGERATE 4 hours or until firm. Unmold. Garnish with remaining grapes and whole strawberries.   *Makes 12 servings*

Nutrition Information Per Serving (using JELL-O Brand Lemon Flavor Sugar Free Low Calorie Gelatin Dessert and orange juice): *60 calories, 0g fat, 0mg cholesterol, 55mg sodium, 9g carbohydrate, 1g dietary fiber, 9g sugars, 1g protein, 35% daily value vitamin C*

Preparation Time: 15 minutes
Refrigerating Time: 4 hours

Gelatin desserts made with wine have long been favorites for elegant entertaining. They are easy to make and impressive to serve. JELL-O gelatin can even trap the bubbles from champagne.

37

Melon Salad

Introduced in the 1990's to appeal to kids, watermelon flavor JELL-O gelatin is popular with grown-ups too. It's especially refreshing with fresh summer fruits.

A wonderful fat free summer refresher.

2½ cups boiling apple juice
  1 package (8-serving size) or 2 packages (4-serving size) JELL-O Brand
      Watermelon Flavor Sugar Free Low Calorie Gelatin Dessert or JELL-O Brand
      Watermelon Flavor Gelatin Dessert
1½ cups cold seltzer or club soda
  1 teaspoon lemon juice
  2 cups cantaloupe and honeydew melon cubes

STIR boiling juice into gelatin in large bowl at least 2 minutes until completely dissolved. Stir in cold seltzer and lemon juice. Refrigerate about 1½ hours or until thickened (spoon drawn through leaves definite impression). Stir in melon cubes. Spoon into 6-cup mold.

REFRIGERATE 4 hours or until firm. Unmold. Garnish as desired.

Makes 10 servings

 Nutrition Information Per Serving (using JELL-O Brand Watermelon Flavor Sugar Free Low Calorie Gelatin Dessert and omitting garnish): *50 calories, 0g fat, 0mg cholesterol, 60mg sodium, 10g carbohydrate, 0g dietary fiber, 10g sugars, 1g protein, 20% daily value vitamin C*

Preparation Time: 15 minutes
Refrigerating Time: 5½ hours

JELL-O *Fun Facts*

In addition to Bill Cosby, famous spokespeople for JELL-O have included Jack Benny, Andy Griffith and Ethel Barrymore.

Melon Salad

Sunset Yogurt Mold

This pineapple-carrot salad, developed in 1977, is one that guests will always appreciate.

2 cups boiling water
1 package (8-serving size) or 2 packages (4-serving size) JELL-O Brand Orange Flavor Sugar Free Low Calorie Gelatin Dessert or JELL-O Brand Orange Flavor Gelatin Dessert
¼ cup cold water
1 can (8 ounces) crushed pineapple in juice, undrained
1 cup grated carrots
1 container (8 ounces) BREYERS Vanilla Lowfat Yogurt

STIR boiling water into gelatin in large bowl at least 2 minutes until completely dissolved. Reserve 1 cup gelatin at room temperature. Stir cold water, pineapple with juice and carrots into remaining gelatin. Spoon into 5-cup mold. Refrigerate about 2 hours or until set but not firm (gelatin should stick to finger when touched and should mound).

STIR yogurt into reserved 1 cup gelatin with wire whisk until smooth. Pour over gelatin layer in mold.

REFRIGERATE 4 hours or until firm. Unmold.   *Makes 10 servings*

 Nutrition Information Per Serving (using JELL-O Brand Orange Flavor Sugar Free Low Calorie Gelatin Dessert): *50 calories, 0g fat, less than 5mg cholesterol, 75mg sodium, 10g carbohydrate, less than 1g dietary fiber, 9g sugars, 3g protein, 70% daily value vitamin A*

Preparation Time: 20 minutes
Refrigerating Time: 6 hours

Waldorf Salad

A delectable molded version of a salad classic.

> **2 cups boiling water**
> **1 package (8-serving size) or 2 packages (4-serving size) JELL-O Brand Lemon**
>   **Flavor Gelatin Dessert**
> **1 cup cold water**
> **1 tablespoon lemon juice**
> **½ cup KRAFT Mayo: Real Mayonnaise or MIRACLE WHIP Salad Dressing**
> **1 medium red apple, diced**
> **½ cup diced celery**
> **¼ cup chopped walnuts**
>   **Salad greens (optional)**

STIR boiling water into gelatin in large bowl at least 2 minutes until completely dissolved. Stir in cold water and lemon juice. Refrigerate about 1½ hours or until thickened (spoon drawn through leaves definite impression). Gradually stir in mayonnaise with wire whisk. Stir in apple, celery and walnuts. Pour into 5-cup mold.

REFRIGERATE 4 hours or until firm. Unmold. Serve on salad greens, if desired.

Makes 10 servings

Preparation Time: 20 minutes
Refrigerating Time: 5½ hours

The original Waldorf salad was created in the 1890's at New York's Waldorf-Astoria Hotel. It consisted of apples, celery and mayonnaise and was served on lettuce. The walnuts were added to the recipe in later years.

JELL-O Fun Facts

A 1908 ad offered a free set of six aluminum molds to JELL-O users. They were directed to buy a package of JELL-O gelatin for 10 cents to learn how to obtain the molds.

Layered Orange Pineapple Mold

This creamy mold with a jewel-like crown goes beautifully with baked ham.

"Congealed" salad molds have long been party and buffet dinner favorites of Southern hostesses.

1 can (20 ounces) crushed pineapple in juice, undrained
Cold water
1½ cups boiling water
1 package (8-serving size) or 2 packages (4-serving size) JELL-O Brand
 Orange Flavor Gelatin Dessert
1 package (8 ounces) PHILADELPHIA BRAND Cream Cheese, softened

DRAIN pineapple, reserving juice. Add cold water to juice to make 1½ cups.

STIR boiling water into gelatin in large bowl at least 2 minutes until completely dissolved. Stir in measured pineapple juice and water. Reserve 1 cup gelatin at room temperature.

STIR ½ of the crushed pineapple into remaining gelatin. Pour into 6-cup mold. Refrigerate about 2 hours or until set but not firm (gelatin should stick to finger when touched and should mound).

STIR reserved 1 cup gelatin gradually into cream cheese in medium bowl with wire whisk until smooth. Stir in remaining crushed pineapple. Pour over gelatin layer in mold.

REFRIGERATE 4 hours or until firm. Unmold. Garnish as desired.

Makes 10 servings

Preparation Time: 20 minutes
Refrigerating Time: 6 hours

43

Layered Orange Pineapple Mold

Creamy Fruited Mold

This simplified version of a classic Bavarian cream offers flavor variations as well as savings in time.

Fluffy and delicious!

1 cup boiling water
1 package (4-serving size) JELL-O Brand Gelatin Dessert, any flavor
1 cup cold water or apple juice
1½ cups thawed COOL WHIP Whipped Topping
1 cup diced fruit

STIR boiling water into gelatin in medium bowl at least 2 minutes until completely dissolved. Stir in cold water. Refrigerate about 1¼ hours or until slightly thickened (consistency of unbeaten egg whites). Gently stir in whipped topping. Refrigerate about 15 minutes or until thickened (spoon drawn through leaves definite impression). Stir in fruit. Pour into 5-cup mold.

REFRIGERATE 4 hours or until firm. Unmold. Garnish as desired. *Makes 8 servings*

Preparation Time: 15 minutes
Refrigerating Time: 5½ hours

1911

Creamy Fruited Mold

Mandarin Orange Mold

JELL-O gelatin molds are good served as either a side dish or dessert. This mold can be served either way.

2 cups boiling water
1 package (8-serving size) or 2 packages (4-serving size) JELL-O Brand Orange Flavor Sugar Free Low Calorie Gelatin Dessert or JELL-O Brand Orange Flavor Gelatin Dessert
¾ cup cold water
1 can (11 ounces) mandarin orange segments in juice, drained
1 container (8 ounces) BREYERS Vanilla Lowfat Yogurt

STIR boiling water into gelatin in large bowl at least 2 minutes until completely dissolved. Reserve 1 cup gelatin at room temperature. Stir cold water and oranges into remaining gelatin. Pour into 5-cup mold. Refrigerate about 2 hours until set but not firm (gelatin should stick to finger when touched and should mound).

STIR yogurt into reserved 1 cup gelatin with wire whisk until smooth. Pour over gelatin layer in mold.

REFRIGERATE 4 hours or until firm. Unmold.   *Makes 10 servings*

 Nutrition Information Per Serving (using JELL-O Brand Orange Flavor Sugar Free Low Calorie Gelatin Dessert): *40 calories, 0g fat, less than 5mg cholesterol, 65mg sodium, 7g carbohydrate, 0g dietary fiber, 6g sugars, 2g protein, 20% daily value vitamin C*

Preparation Time: 20 minutes
Refrigerating Time: 6 hours

Three Pepper Salad with Salsa Sauce

A confetti-like salad mold with a zesty contrasting sauce.

2 cups boiling water
1 package (8-serving size) or 2 packages (4-serving size) JELL-O Brand Lemon
    Flavor Gelatin Dessert
1½ cups cold water
2 tablespoons lemon juice
2 cups chopped red, green and/or yellow peppers
2 tablespoons sliced green onions
    Salsa Sauce (recipe follows)

This salad reflects America's love for salsa, which has overtaken ketchup as the most popular condiment.

STIR boiling water into gelatin in large bowl at least 2 minutes until completely dissolved. Stir in cold water and lemon juice. Refrigerate about 1½ hours or until thickened (spoon drawn through leaves definite impression). Stir in peppers and onions. Pour into 5-cup mold.

REFRIGERATE 4 hours or until firm. Unmold. Serve with Salsa Sauce.

Makes 10 servings

Salsa Sauce: Mix ½ cup *each* KRAFT Mayo: Real Mayonnaise, BREAKSTONE'S Sour Cream and salsa until blended.

Preparation Time: 20 minutes
Refrigerating Time: 5½ hours

The very first color ad for JELL-O depicted the JELL-O Girl making and serving the product. Also featured in the ad were a number of beautiful molds, such as Tomato Salad JELL-O, Neapolitan JELL-O, Chocolate Walnut JELL-O and Wine JELL-O.

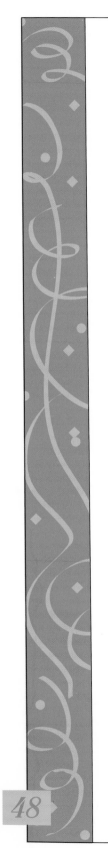

Snack Attacks

There are snacks in this chapter to suit every taste, from JIGGLERS® for kids to Pudding Café for the more sophisticated palate. All are fun to make and eat and keep well in the refrigerator or freezer—ready to come to the rescue when a snack attack occurs.

Many feature the wholesomeness of milk, yogurt and fruit; some conceal surprise taste treats; and others are especially refreshing. There are finger foods, cups, parfaits, pops, sherbets, frozen squares and cookiewiches, mini cheesecakes, and drinks—any one of which will pleasantly satisfy until the next meal comes around.

Clockwise from top left: Rocky Road Pudding Chillers and Cookies & Cream Pudding Chillers (page 67), Pudding in a Cloud (page 55), JIGGLERS® (page 50), Creamy JIGGLERS® (page 66)

49

Chocolate Peanut Butter Parfaits

In the 1950's JELL-O instant pudding was advertised on these network television shows: Our Miss Brooks, Red Buttons, Rocket Rangers, Roy Rogers *and* The Bob Hope Show.

Yummm! Luscious layers of two favorite flavors.

3 tablespoons milk
3 tablespoons peanut butter
1 cup thawed COOL WHIP Whipped Topping
2 cups cold milk
1 package (4-serving size) JELL-O Chocolate Flavor Instant
    Pudding & Pie Filling
¼ cup chopped peanuts

STIR 3 tablespoons milk into peanut butter in medium bowl until smooth. Gently stir in whipped topping.

POUR 2 cups milk into medium bowl. Add pudding mix. Beat with wire whisk 2 minutes. Alternately spoon whipped topping mixture and pudding into 6 parfait glasses.

REFRIGERATE until ready to serve. Sprinkle with peanuts.   *Makes 6 servings*

Preparation Time: 15 minutes

JIGGLERS®

Introduced in 1989, wiggly JELL-O JIGGLERS® is the most requested JELL-O recipe ever, according to the company's Consumer Response Center.

Fabulous fun finger foods that kids adore!

2½ cups boiling water or boiling apple juice (Do not add cold water or cold juice.)
    2 packages (8-serving size) or 4 packages (4-serving size) JELL-O Brand Gelatin
        Dessert, any flavor

STIR boiling water or boiling juice into gelatin in large bowl at least 3 minutes until completely dissolved. Pour into 13×9-inch pan.

REFRIGERATE 3 hours or until firm. Dip bottom of pan in warm water about 15 seconds. Cut into decorative shapes with cookie cutters all the way through gelatin or cut into 1-inch squares. Lift from pan.   *Makes about 24 pieces*

Note: *Recipe can be halved. Use 8- or 9-inch square pan.*

Preparation Time: 10 minutes
Refrigerating Time: 3 hours

Chocolate Peanut Butter Parfaits

Aquarium Cups

Berry Blue was introduced in 1992. Recipes like Aquarium Cups have helped to popularize this fun flavor. More than 21 million packages of Berry Blue were sold in its first year.

¾ **cup boiling water**
1 **package (4-serving size) JELL-O Brand Berry Blue Flavor Gelatin Dessert**
½ **cup cold water**
  Ice cubes
  Gummy fish

STIR boiling water into gelatin in medium bowl at least 2 minutes until completely dissolved. Mix cold water and ice cubes to make 1¼ cups. Add to gelatin, stirring until slightly thickened. Remove any remaining ice. (If mixture is still thin, refrigerate until slightly thickened.)

POUR thickened gelatin into 4 dessert dishes. Suspend gummy fish in gelatin. Refrigerate 1 hour or until firm. *Makes 4 servings*

Preparation Time: 10 minutes
Refrigerating Time: 1 hour

Refreshers

1 **cup boiling water**
1 **package (4-serving size) JELL-O Brand Gelatin Dessert, any flavor**
1 **cup cold beverage, such as seltzer, club soda, ginger ale, iced tea or lemon-lime**
  carbonated beverage

STIR boiling water into gelatin in medium bowl at least 2 minutes until completely dissolved. Stir in cold beverage.

REFRIGERATE 4 hours or until firm. Cut into cubes and garnish as desired.
Makes 4 servings

Sugar Free Low Calorie Refreshers: Prepare recipe as directed above using any flavor JELL-O Brand Sugar Free Low Calorie Gelatin Dessert and 1 cup seltzer, club soda, diet ginger ale, diet iced tea or diet lemon-lime carbonated beverage.

 Nutrition Information Per Serving (for Sugar Free Low Calorie Refreshers, omitting garnish): *10 calories, 0g fat, 0mg cholesterol, 90mg sodium, 0g carbohydrate, 0g dietary fiber, 0g sugars, 1g protein*

Preparation Time: 5 minutes
Refrigerating Time: 4 hours

53

Refreshers

Frozen Pudding COOKIEWICHES™

This peanut butter and pudding recipe also works well with chocolate wafers.

Keep these treats on hand in the freezer for last-minute snacks.

1½ cups cold milk
½ cup peanut butter
1 package (4-serving size) JELL-O Instant Pudding & Pie Filling, any flavor
24 graham crackers
Colored sprinkles

STIR milk gradually into peanut butter in deep narrow bottom bowl until smooth. Add pudding mix. Beat with wire whisk 2 minutes. Let stand 5 minutes.

SPREAD pudding mixture about ½-inch thick onto 12 of the crackers. Top with remaining crackers, pressing lightly and smoothing around edges with spatula. Coat edges with sprinkles.

FREEZE 3 hours or until firm.   *Makes 12*

Preparation Time: 15 minutes
Freezing Time: 3 hours

Pudding Café

Flavor your pudding to fit your mood—Irish, Cappuccino, Mocha or Amaretto.

The addition of flavored coffees to this creamy snack makes it a favorite with adults.

2 cups cold milk
1 package (4-serving size) JELL-O Chocolate or Vanilla Flavor Instant
    Pudding & Pie Filling
¼ cup GENERAL FOODS INTERNATIONAL COFFEES, any flavor

POUR milk into medium bowl. Add pudding mix and flavored instant coffee. Beat with wire whisk 2 minutes. Refrigerate until ready to serve.   *Makes 4 servings*

Preparation Time: 5 minutes
Refrigerating Time: 2 hours

JIGGLERS® *Snack Pops*

JIGGLERS® *on sticks—like lollipops!*

1¼ cups boiling water
1 package (8-serving size) or 2 packages (4-serving size) JELL-O Brand Gelatin
**   Dessert, any flavor**
4 (5-ounce) paper cups
6 plastic straws, cut in half

STIR boiling water into gelatin in medium bowl at least 3 minutes until completely dissolved. Cool 15 minutes at room temperature. Pour into cups.

REFRIGERATE 3 hours or until firm. Carefully peel away cups. Using a knife dipped in warm water, cut each gelatin cup horizontally into 3 round slices. Insert straw into each gelatin slice to resemble a lollipop.   *Makes 12 pops*

Preparation Time: 10 minutes
Refrigerating Time: 3 hours

Kids will love these pops made with such kid flavors as Berry Blue, Black Cherry, Grape and Watermelon.

Pudding in a Cloud

How to please the family in just 15 minutes.

2 cups thawed COOL WHIP Whipped Topping
2 cups cold milk
1 package (4-serving size) JELL-O Instant Pudding & Pie Filling, any flavor

SPOON whipped topping evenly into 6 dessert dishes. Using back of spoon, spread whipped topping onto bottom and up side of each dish.

POUR milk into medium bowl. Add pudding mix. Beat with wire whisk 2 minutes. Let stand 5 minutes. Spoon pudding into center of whipped topping.

REFRIGERATE until ready to serve.   *Makes 6 servings*

Preparation Time: 15 minutes
Refrigerating Time: 2 hours

Amuse the kids by letting them make faces on the pudding with pieces of marshmallow, gumdrops or decorating gel.

 Fruity Gelatin Pops

These super after-school treats couldn't be easier!

1 cup boiling water
1 package (4-serving size) JELL-O Brand Gelatin Dessert, any flavor
½ cup sugar
2 cups cold water
7 (5-ounce) paper cups

STIR boiling water into gelatin and sugar in medium bowl at least 2 minutes until completely dissolved. Stir in cold water. Pour into cups. Freeze about 2 hours or until almost firm. Insert wooden pop stick into each for handle.

FREEZE 5 hours or overnight until firm. To remove pop from cup, place bottom of cup under warm running water for 15 seconds. Press firmly on bottom of cup to release pop. (Do not twist or pull pop stick.)   *Makes 7 pops*

Iced Tea Pops: Use 1 cup boiling water, JELL-O Brand Lemon Flavor Gelatin Dessert, ¼ cup sugar and 2 cups pre-sweetened iced tea.

Strawberry Pops: Use 1 cup boiling water, JELL-O Brand Strawberry Flavor Gelatin Dessert, ½ cup sugar, 1 cup cold water and 1 cup puréed strawberries.

Lemonade Pops: Use 1 cup boiling water, JELL-O Brand Lemon Flavor Gelatin Dessert, ½ cup sugar, 1¾ cups cold water and ¼ cup lemon juice.

Orange Pops: Use 1 cup boiling water, JELL-O Brand Orange Flavor Gelatin Dessert, ½ cup sugar and 2 cups orange juice.

Preparation Time: 10 minutes
Freezing Time: 7 hours

In the 1930's, JELL-O sponsored a Wizard of Oz radio program and published a series of children's booklets by Frank L. Baum. Some of the titles were The Scarecrow and the Tin Woodman, Jack Pumpkinhead and the Sawhorse, Ozma and the Little Wizard, *and* Tiktok and the NomeKing.

56

57

Top to bottom: Lemonade Pops, Orange Pops

Fresh Fruit Parfaits

Experiment with gelatin-fruit combinations such as orange flavor gelatin with fresh peaches; lime flavor with melon balls; or strawberry flavor with strawberries, bananas and/or blueberries.

Whip up these fat free layered parfaits tonight!

1 cup fresh fruit
¾ cup boiling water
1 package (4-serving size) JELL-O Brand Sugar Free Low Calorie Gelatin Dessert or JELL-O Brand Gelatin Dessert, any flavor
½ cup cold water
Ice cubes
¾ cup thawed COOL WHIP FREE or COOL WHIP LITE Whipped Topping

DIVIDE fruit among 6 parfait glasses.

STIR boiling water into gelatin in medium bowl at least 2 minutes until completely dissolved. Mix cold water and ice cubes to make 1¼ cups. Add to gelatin, stirring until slightly thickened. Remove any remaining ice. Measure ¾ cup of the gelatin; pour into parfait glasses. Refrigerate 1 hour or until set but not firm (gelatin should stick to finger when touched and should mound).

STIR whipped topping into remaining gelatin with wire whisk until smooth. Spoon over gelatin in glasses.

REFRIGERATE 1 hour or until firm. Garnish as desired.   *Makes 6 servings*

 Nutrition Information Per Serving (using ½ cup each blueberries and strawberries, JELL-O Brand Sugar Free Low Calorie Gelatin Dessert and COOL WHIP FREE and omitting cookies): 35 calories, 0.5g fat, 0mg cholesterol, 55mg sodium, 6g carbohydrate, less than 1g dietary fiber, 3g sugars, 1g protein, 15% daily value vitamin C

Preparation Time: 20 minutes
Refrigerating Time: 2 hours

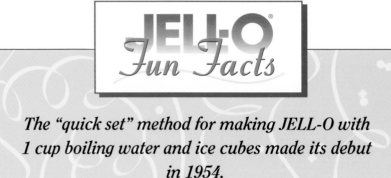

JELL-O® Fun Facts

The "quick set" method for making JELL-O with 1 cup boiling water and ice cubes made its debut in 1954.

Fresh Fruit Parfaits

Florida Sunshine Cups

Serve this refreshing fat free snack any time of day.

1 cup boiling water
1 package (4-serving size) JELL-O Brand Orange or Lemon Flavor Sugar Free Low Calorie Gelatin Dessert or JELL-O Brand Orange or Lemon Flavor Gelatin Dessert
¾ cup cold water
½ cup fresh grapefruit sections, halved
½ cup fresh orange sections, halved

STIR boiling water into gelatin in large bowl at least 2 minutes until completely dissolved. Stir in cold water. Reserve ¾ cup gelatin in medium bowl at room temperature. Refrigerate remaining gelatin about 45 minutes or until thickened (spoon drawn through leaves definite impression). Stir in fruit. Pour into serving bowl or 6 dessert dishes. Refrigerate about 10 minutes or until firm (gelatin should stick to finger when touched and should mound).

MEANWHILE, place reserved gelatin in larger bowl of ice and water. Stir until slightly thickened. Beat at high speed of electric mixer until thick and about doubled in volume. Spoon over gelatin in bowl or dishes.

REFRIGERATE 1 hour or until firm.   *Makes 6 servings*

 Nutrition Information Per Serving (using JELL-O Brand Orange Flavor Sugar Free Low Calorie Gelatin Dessert): *20 calories, 0g fat, 0mg cholesterol, 45mg sodium, 3g carbohydrate, less than 1g dietary fiber, 2g sugars, 1g protein, 25% daily value vitamin C*

Preparation Time: 20 minutes
Refrigerating Time: 2 hours

Strawberry Banana Smoothie

Satisfy the between-meal "hungries" with this yummy drink.

> **2 cups crushed ice**
> **1 cup cold milk**
> **1 package (4-serving size) JELL-O Brand Strawberry Flavor Gelatin Dessert**
> **1 container (8 ounces) BREYERS Vanilla Lowfat Yogurt**
> **1 large banana, cut into chunks**

A great shake made with bananas, low fat yogurt and JELL-O Brand Gelatin.

PLACE all ingredients in blender container; cover. Blend on high speed 30 seconds or until smooth. Serve immediately.   *Makes 4 servings*

Preparation Time: 5 minutes

Strawberry Sorbet

Full of fruit flavor, this refreshing sorbet will melt in your mouth.

> **1 package (10 ounces) frozen strawberries in syrup, thawed**
> **1 cup cold water**
> **2 cups boiling water**
> **1 package (4-serving size) JELL-O Brand Strawberry Flavor Gelatin Dessert**
> **¾ cup sugar**

PLACE strawberries and cold water in blender container; cover. Blend on high speed until smooth.

STIR boiling water into gelatin and sugar in large bowl at least 2 minutes until completely dissolved. Stir in strawberry mixture. Pour into 9-inch square pan.

FREEZE about 1 hour or until ice crystals form 1 inch around edges. Spoon into blender container; cover. Blend on high speed about 30 seconds or until smooth. Return to pan.

FREEZE 6 hours or overnight until firm. Scoop into dessert dishes.

Makes 10 servings

Preparation Time: 15 minutes
Freezing Time: 7 hours

Dirt Cups

This recipe was developed in 1989 as part of the JELL-O Snacktivities® campaign to encourage parents and kids to make fun recipes together.

Great kid appeal here!

1 package (16 ounces) chocolate sandwich cookies
2 cups cold milk
1 package (4-serving size) JELL-O Chocolate Flavor Instant Pudding & Pie Filling
1 tub (8 ounces) COOL WHIP Whipped Topping, thawed
8 to 10 (7-ounce) paper or plastic cups
   Suggested garnishes: gummy worms or other gummy candies, candy flowers, chopped peanuts, granola

CRUSH cookies in zipper-style plastic bag with rolling pin or in food processor.

POUR milk into large bowl. Add pudding mix. Beat with wire whisk 2 minutes. Stir in whipped topping and ½ of the crushed cookies.

PLACE about 1 tablespoon of the crushed cookies in each cup. Fill cups about ¾ full with pudding mixture. Top with remaining crushed cookies.

REFRIGERATE until ready to serve. Garnish as desired.   *Makes 8 to 10 servings*

Sand Cups: Use 1 package (12 ounces) vanilla wafer cookies and JELL-O Vanilla Flavor Instant Pudding & Pie Filling.

Preparation Time: 15 minutes
Refrigerating Time: 2 hours

Some New Ideas

Shouts of "Oh, Good-e-e-e!" and clapping of hands greet mamma's appearance with a big dish of Jell-O for Bobbie and Jack.

It is a plain dish of Strawberry Jell-O, made and served without sugar or cream—but perfectly delicious.

Substantial dishes that are good to eat and generally made without any trimmings or garnishments, are very popular just now. Probably the Bavarian creams made as follows are the most satisfactory:

Dissolve a package of Lemon Jell-O in half a pint of boiling water and add half a pint of the juice from a can of pineapple. When cold and still liquid whip to consistency of whipped cream and add a cup of shredded or chopped pineapple.

Either fresh or canned fruit of almost any other kind can be used in making these Bavarian creams. Canned peaches and peach juice are particularly good.

The whipped Jell-O takes the place of whipped cream in these dishes, and no eggs are used in them. Anybody can make them.

In every case of sickness or convalescence there is a period when feeding is a most important factor, and often it is found that Jell-O is the one particular dish which satisfies the craving for something refreshing and revives the weakened appetite. It is relished when nothing else is.

The Jell-O Book contains a special recipe for whipping Jell-O, which is a simple process. If you have not already received a copy of this book we shall be glad to send you one if you will give us your name and address.

Jell-O is put up in six pure fruit flavors: Strawberry, Raspberry, Lemon, Orange, Cherry, Chocolate, and is sold by all grocers, 2 packages for 25 cents.

THE GENESEE PURE FOOD COMPANY,
Le Roy, N. Y., and Bridgeburg, Ont.

JELL-O

1918

63

Left to right: Sand Cups, Dirt Cups

Miniature Cheesecakes

Add a candle to each of these desserts for a quick birthday party treat.

1 package (11.1 ounces) JELL-O No Bake Real Cheesecake
2 tablespoons sugar
⅓ cup butter or margarine, melted
1½ cups cold milk
2 squares BAKER'S Semi-Sweet Baking Chocolate, melted (optional)

MIX crumbs, sugar and butter thoroughly with fork in medium bowl until crumbs are well moistened. Press onto bottoms of 12 paper-lined or foil-lined muffin cups.

BEAT milk and filling mix with electric mixer on low speed until blended. Beat on medium speed 3 minutes. (Filling will be thick.) Spoon over crumb mixture in muffin cups. Drizzle with melted chocolate, if desired.

REFRIGERATE at least 1 hour or until ready to serve. Garnish as desired.

Makes 12 servings

Preparation Time: 15 minutes
Refrigerating Time: 1 hour

Cinnamon Chocolate Pudding

A low fat treat with plenty of flavor.

2 cups cold skim milk
1 package (4-serving size) JELL-O Devil's Food Flavor Fat Free Instant Pudding & Pie Filling or JELL-O Chocolate Flavor Instant Pudding & Pie Filling
½ teaspoon ground cinnamon
½ cup thawed COOL WHIP FREE or COOL WHIP LITE Whipped Topping

POUR milk into medium bowl. Add pudding mix and cinnamon. Beat with wire whisk 1 minute. Gently stir in whipped topping. Spoon into dessert dishes.

REFRIGERATE until ready to serve.

Makes 5 servings

 Nutrition Information Per Serving (using JELL-O Devil's Food Flavor Fat Free Instant Pudding & Pie Filling and COOL WHIP FREE): *130 calories, 1g fat, 0mg cholesterol, 340mg sodium, 28g carbohydrate, less than 1g dietary fiber, 4g protein, 10% daily value calcium*

Preparation Time: 5 minutes
Refrigerating Time: 2 hours

Miniature Cheesecakes

Buried Treasures

This is a great recipe to make with children, who will have fun selecting the "treasures."

2 cups cold milk
1 package (4-serving size) JELL-O Instant Pudding & Pie Filling, any flavor
Assorted "treasures": BAKER'S Semi-Sweet Real Chocolate Chips, chopped nuts, miniature marshmallows, raisins, chopped bananas, halved grapes, crumbled chocolate sandwich cookies or peanut butter
Thawed COOL WHIP Whipped Topping

POUR milk into medium bowl. Add pudding mix. Beat with wire whisk 2 minutes.

PLACE 1 tablespoon of the "treasures" into each of 4 dessert glasses. Spoon pudding over treasures.

REFRIGERATE until ready to serve. Top with whipped topping and garnish as desired.
Makes 4 servings

Preparation Time: 15 minutes
Refrigerating Time: 2 hours

Creamy JIGGLERS®

JIGGLERS® are as much fun for kids' parties today as mini JELL-O molds were for birthday celebrations in the 1920's. A 1925 JELL-O ad called "Mine's Best," showed three girls in party dresses and three boys in suits, each holding a different flavor JELL-O.

2½ cups boiling water
2 packages (8-serving size) or 4 packages (4-serving size) JELL-O Brand Gelatin Dessert, any flavor
1 cup cold milk
1 package (4-serving size) JELL-O Vanilla Flavor Instant Pudding & Pie Filling

STIR boiling water into gelatin in large bowl at least 3 minutes until completely dissolved. Cool 30 minutes at room temperature.

POUR milk into medium bowl. Add pudding mix. Beat with wire whisk 1 minute. Quickly pour into gelatin. Stir with wire whisk until well blended. Pour into 13×9-inch pan.

REFRIGERATE 3 hours or until firm. Dip bottom of pan in warm water about 15 seconds. Cut into decorative shapes with cookie cutters all the way through gelatin or cut into 1-inch squares. Lift from pan.
Makes about 24 pieces

Preparation Time: 15 minutes
Refrigerating Time: 3 hours

66

Pudding Chillers

After school is the perfect time for savoring these frozen pops.

2 cups cold milk
1 package (4-serving size) JELL-O Instant Pudding & Pie Filling, any flavor
6 (5-ounce) paper cups

POUR milk into medium bowl. Add pudding mix. Beat with wire whisk 2 minutes. Spoon into cups. Insert wooden pop stick into each for a handle.

FREEZE 5 hours or overnight until firm. To remove pop from cup, place bottom of cup under warm running water for 15 seconds. Press firmly on bottom of cup to release pop. (Do not twist or pull pop stick.)   *Makes 6 pops*

Rocky Road: Use JELL-O Chocolate Flavor Instant Pudding & Pie Filling and stir in ½ cup miniature marshmallows and ¼ cup *each* BAKER'S Semi-Sweet Real Chocolate Chips and chopped peanuts.

Toffee Crunch: Use JELL-O Vanilla Flavor Instant Pudding & Pie Filling and stir in ½ cup chopped chocolate-covered toffee bars.

Cookies & Cream: Use JELL-O Vanilla Flavor Instant Pudding & Pie Filling and stir in ½ cup chopped chocolate sandwich cookies.

Preparation Time: 10 minutes
Freezing Time: 5 hours

Experiment with other mix-ins, such as crushed peppermint candy, chunky peanut butter, chopped or mashed fruit, chocolate sprinkles, swirls of jam or ice cream toppings.

The Butler Serves and the Housewife Too

JELL-O

1918

Pudding Mousse

Mousse, a French term for "froth" or "foam," is traditionally a rich mixture fluffed up with whipped cream.

1½ cups cold milk
1 package (4-serving size) JELL-O Instant Pudding & Pie Filling, any flavor
1½ cups thawed COOL WHIP Whipped Topping

POUR milk into large bowl. Add pudding mix. Beat with wire whisk 2 minutes.

STIR in 1 cup of the whipped topping. Spoon into individual dessert dishes or serving bowl.

REFRIGERATE until ready to serve. Top with remaining whipped topping and garnish as desired.
Makes 5 servings

Low Fat Pudding Mousse: Prepare recipe as directed above using skim milk, any flavor JELL-O Fat Free Sugar Free Instant Reduced Calorie Pudding & Pie Filling and COOL WHIP FREE or COOL WHIP LITE Whipped Topping.

 Nutrition Information Per Serving (for Low Fat Pudding Mousse, using JELL-O Chocolate Flavor Fat Free Sugar Free Instant Reduced Calorie Pudding & Pie Filling and COOL WHIP FREE and omitting garnish): 90 calories, 1.5g fat, 0mg cholesterol, 300mg sodium, 18g carbohydrate, less than 1g dietary fiber, 7g sugars, 3g protein, 10% daily value calcium

Preparation Time: 5 minutes
Refrigerating Time: 2 hours

JELL-O
America's most famous dessert.

1926

Pudding Mousse

69

Yogurt Fluff

Versatile yogurt adds creamy smoothness to this ever-so-simple low fat treat.

JELL-O gelatin has always been naturally fat free and pairing it with low fat yogurt makes a delightful combination.

¾ **cup boiling water**
1 **package (4-serving size) JELL-O Brand Sugar Free Low Calorie Gelatin Dessert or JELL-O Brand Gelatin Dessert, any flavor**
½ **cup cold water or fruit juice**
  Ice cubes
1 **container (8 ounces) BREYERS Vanilla Lowfat Yogurt**
½ **teaspoon vanilla (optional)**
5 **tablespoons thawed COOL WHIP FREE or COOL WHIP LITE Whipped Topping**

STIR boiling water into gelatin in large bowl at least 2 minutes until completely dissolved.

MIX cold water and ice cubes to make 1 cup. Add to gelatin, stirring until slightly thickened. Remove any remaining ice. Stir in yogurt and vanilla. Pour into dessert dishes.

REFRIGERATE 1½ hours or until firm. Top with whipped topping.

Makes 5 servings

 Nutrition Information Per Serving (using JELL-O Brand Sugar Free Low Calorie Gelatin Dessert, water and COOL WHIP FREE): *60 calories, 1g fat, less than 5mg cholesterol, 90mg sodium, 9g carbohydrate, 0g dietary fiber, 8g sugars, 3g protein*

Preparation Time: 10 minutes
Refrigerating Time: 1½ hours

71

Yogurt Fluff

Creamy Orange Shake

JELL-O gelatin adds flavor and body to this delicious drink.

This frosty shake is sure to become a favorite after-school snack.

1 cup cold milk
1 cup orange juice
1 package (4-serving size) JELL-O Brand Orange Flavor Gelatin Dessert
1 cup vanilla ice cream

POUR milk and juice into blender container. Add gelatin and ice cream; cover. Blend on high speed 30 seconds or until smooth. Serve immediately.

Makes 4 servings

Preparation Time: 5 minutes

Chocolate Banana Split

2 cups cold skim milk
1 package (4-serving size) JELL-O Chocolate Flavor Fat Free Sugar Free Instant Reduced Calorie Pudding & Pie Filling or JELL-O Chocolate Flavor Instant Pudding & Pie Filling
2 medium bananas, sliced
½ cup thawed COOL WHIP FREE or COOL WHIP LITE Whipped Topping
1 tablespoon chopped walnuts

POUR milk into medium bowl. Add pudding mix. Beat with wire whisk 2 minutes.

SPOON ½ of the pudding evenly into 4 dessert dishes. Layer with banana slices. Spoon remaining pudding over bananas.

REFRIGERATE until ready to serve. Top each serving with 2 tablespoons whipped topping. Sprinkle with walnuts.

Makes 4 servings

 Nutrition Information Per Serving (using JELL-O Chocolate Flavor Fat Free Sugar Free Instant Reduced Calorie Pudding & Pie Filling and COOL WHIP FREE):
160 calories, 2.5g fat, less than 5mg cholesterol, 380mg sodium, 31g carbohydrate, 2g dietary fiber, 16g sugars, 6g protein, 15% daily value calcium

Preparation Time: 10 minutes
Refrigerating Time: 2 hours

Peanut Butter and JELL-O Parfaits

An all-time favorite flavor combination.

2 cups boiling water
1 package (8-serving size) or 2 packages (4-serving size) JELL-O Brand Grape Flavor Gelatin Dessert
1 cup cold water
1 cup cold milk
½ cup creamy peanut butter
1 package (4-serving size) JELL-O Vanilla Flavor Instant Pudding & Pie Filling
1 cup thawed COOL WHIP Whipped Topping

STIR boiling water into gelatin in medium bowl at least 2 minutes until completely dissolved. Stir in cold water. Pour into 13×9-inch pan. Refrigerate 3 hours or until firm. Cut gelatin into ½-inch cubes.

STIR milk gradually into peanut butter in medium bowl until smooth. Add pudding mix. Beat with electric mixer on medium speed 2 minutes. Gently stir in whipped topping. Layer gelatin cubes alternately with peanut butter mixture in 6 parfait glasses, ending with gelatin cubes.

REFRIGERATE until ready to serve.   *Makes 6 servings*

Preparation Time: 20 minutes
Refrigerating Time: 3 hours

A 1925 booklet called "The JELL-O Girl Entertains" included exercises for children and "New and Interesting Games," including Balloon Tennis, Feather Blowing Game and Making Clown Faces.

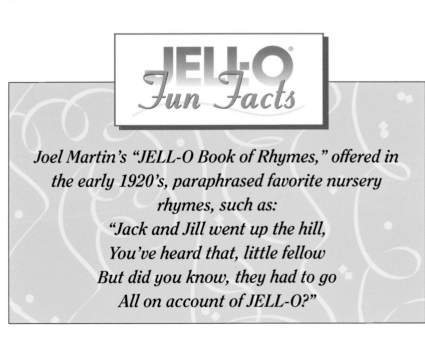

JELL-O® Fun Facts

Joel Martin's "JELL-O Book of Rhymes," offered in the early 1920's, paraphrased favorite nursery rhymes, such as:
"Jack and Jill went up the hill,
You've heard that, little fellow
But did you know, they had to go
All on account of JELL-O?"

Easy Pudding Milk Shake

In just minutes, you can whip up this creamy milk shake—enough for the entire family.

This milk shake will thicken as it stands. To thin shake, just add more milk. To make one serving, use 1 cup milk, 1 scoop ice cream and 3 tablespoons instant pudding.

3 cups cold milk
1 package (4-serving size) JELL-O Instant Pudding & Pie Filling, any flavor
1½ cups ice cream, any flavor

POUR milk into blender container. Add pudding mix and ice cream; cover. Blend on high speed 30 seconds or until smooth. Pour into glasses and garnish as desired. Serve immediately.   *Makes 5 servings*

Preparation Time: 5 minutes

Gelatin Pinwheels

Let the kids help make these—it's fun!

These snacks are truly magical because the melted marshmallows float to the top of the gelatin mixture, forming a contrasting creamy swirl when rolled up.

1 package (4-serving size) JELL-O Brand Gelatin Dessert, any flavor
½ cup warm water
1½ cups miniature marshmallows or 12 large marshmallows

SPRAY bottom and sides of 8- or 9-inch square pan lightly with no stick cooking spray.

MIX gelatin and water in 1½- to 2-quart microwavable bowl. Microwave on HIGH 1½ minutes; stir until completely dissolved. Add marshmallows. Microwave 1 minute or until marshmallows are puffed and almost melted. Remove from oven. Stir mixture slowly and gently until marshmallows are completely melted and mixture is smooth. (Creamy layer will float to top.) Pour into prepared pan.

REFRIGERATE 45 minutes or until set. Loosen edges with knife. Starting at 1 edge, roll up tightly. With seam-side down, cut into ½-inch slices.

SERVE immediately or refrigerate until ready to serve.   *Makes 10 to 12 pieces*

Preparation Time: 10 minutes
Refrigerating Time: 45 minutes

74

Easy Pudding Milk Shakes

All-Time Favorites

Many of us recall favorite JELL-O salads and desserts from our childhood. This chapter contains classic recipes, most of which have been around for at least a generation or two or have been frequently requested. In some cases, recipe titles have been changed from the originals.

The Kraft Consumer Response Center receives about 12,000 requests for JELL-O recipes each year. Currently at the top of the list are Gelatin Poke Cake, Under-the-Sea Salad, Vanilla Rice Pudding and Watergate Salad.

Try these time-tested creations on your family and guests. You'll soon discover why these are still consumers' favorite recipes.

*Top to bottom: Vanilla Rice Pudding (page 92), Chocolate Swirl Cheesecake (page 80),
Under-the-Sea Salad (page 86), Ribbon Squares (page 81)*

77

Crown Jewel Dessert

Shimmering gems of JELL-O make this mold extra special.

The concept of creamy gelatin with clear cubes originated in 1955 with a recipe called Broken Window Glass Cake.

1 package (4-serving size) JELL-O Brand Lime Flavor Gelatin Dessert*
1 package (4-serving size) JELL-O Brand Orange Flavor Gelatin Dessert*
1 package (4-serving size) JELL-O Brand Strawberry Flavor Gelatin Dessert*
3 cups boiling water
1½ cups cold water
1 cup boiling water
1 package (4-serving size) JELL-O Brand Strawberry Flavor Gelatin Dessert
½ cup cold water
1 tub (8 ounces) COOL WHIP Whipped Topping, thawed

PREPARE lime, orange and 1 package strawberry gelatin separately as directed on packages, using 1 cup boiling water and ½ cup cold water for each. Pour each flavor into separate 8-inch square pans. Refrigerate 4 hours or until firm. Cut into ½-inch cubes; measure 1½ cups of each flavor. (Use remaining gelatin cubes for garnish if desired or for snacking.)

STIR 1 cup boiling water into remaining package of strawberry gelatin in medium bowl at least 2 minutes until completely dissolved. Stir in ½ cup cold water. Refrigerate 45 minutes or until slightly thickened (consistency of unbeaten egg whites).

STIR in ½ of the whipped topping. Gently stir in measured gelatin cubes. Pour into 9×5-inch loaf pan.

REFRIGERATE 4 hours or until firm. Unmold. Garnish with remaining whipped topping and gelatin cubes, if desired. *Makes 16 servings*

*Or use any 3 different flavors of JELL-O Brand Gelatin Dessert.

Preparation Time: 45 minutes
Refrigerating Time: 8¾ hours

Crown Jewel Dessert

*C*hocolate Swirl Cheesecake

Originally developed in 1966 for the introduction of JELL-O No Bake Cheesecake, this glamorous dessert looks as though it took hours to prepare.

Create this elegant showpiece dessert in just minutes.

1 package (11.1 ounces) JELL-O No Bake Real Cheesecake
2 tablespoons sugar
⅓ cup butter or margarine, melted
2 squares BAKER'S Semi-Sweet Baking Chocolate
1½ cups cold milk, divided

MIX crumbs, sugar and butter thoroughly with fork in 9-inch pie plate until crumbs are well moistened. Press firmly against side of pie plate first, using finger or large spoon to shape edge. Press remaining crumbs firmly onto bottom using measuring cup.

MICROWAVE chocolate and 2 tablespoons of the milk in microwavable bowl on HIGH 1½ minutes or until chocolate is almost melted. Stir until chocolate is completely melted.

BEAT remaining milk and filling mix with electric mixer on low speed until blended. Beat on medium speed 3 minutes. (Filling will be thick.) Spoon 2 cups of the filling into crust. Stir chocolate mixture into remaining filling. Spoon over cheesecake. Swirl with knife to marbleize.

REFRIGERATE at least 1 hour.

Makes 8 servings

Preparation Time: 15 minutes
Refrigerating Time: 1 hour

1921

*R*ibbon Squares

Impress friends and family alike with this colorful three-layer salad.

> **3 cups boiling water**
> **1 package (4-serving size) JELL-O Brand Gelatin Dessert, any red flavor**
> **1 package (4-serving size) JELL-O Brand Lemon Flavor Gelatin Dessert**
> **1 package (4-serving size) JELL-O Brand Lime Flavor Gelatin Dessert**
> **1½ cups cold water**
> **1 package (8 ounces) PHILADELPHIA BRAND Cream Cheese, softened**
> **1 can (8 ounces) crushed pineapple in juice, undrained**
> **1 cup thawed COOL WHIP Whipped Topping**
> **½ cup KRAFT Mayo: Real Mayonnaise**

STIR 1 cup boiling water into each flavor of gelatin in separate medium bowls at least 2 minutes until completely dissolved. Stir ¾ cup of the cold water into red gelatin. Pour into 9-inch square pan. Refrigerate about 45 minutes or until set but not firm (gelatin should stick to finger when touched and should mound).

MEANWHILE, stir lemon gelatin gradually into cream cheese in large bowl with wire whisk until smooth. Stir in pineapple with juice. Refrigerate about 45 minutes or until slightly thickened (consistency of unbeaten egg whites). Stir in whipped topping and mayonnaise. Spoon over red gelatin layer in pan. Refrigerate about 30 minutes or until set but not firm (gelatin should stick to finger when touched and should mound).

MEANWHILE, stir remaining ¾ cup cold water into lime gelatin. Refrigerate about 30 minutes or until slightly thickened (consistency of unbeaten egg whites). Spoon over lemon gelatin mixture in pan.

REFRIGERATE 4 hours or until firm. Unmold. Cut into squares. Garnish as desired.

Makes 9 servings

Preparation Time: 30 minutes
Refrigerating Time: 5¼ hours

Canned pineapple works perfectly in gelatin salads and desserts. Fresh pineapple, however, contains an enzyme that prevents gelatin from setting so it should never be used as an ingredient when preparing JELL-O.

Saucy Bake

Having originated more than 20 years ago, this moist cake-topped dessert is a family favorite, making enough for second helpings.

Pudding and cake both in one easy-to-fix dessert.

> 1 package (2-layer size) yellow or devil's food cake mix or cake mix with pudding in the mix
> 2 cups water
> 2 cups milk
> 2 packages (4-serving size) JELL-O Chocolate Flavor Instant Pudding & Pie Filling
> ⅓ cup sugar
> ¼ to ½ teaspoon ground cinnamon

HEAT oven to 350°F.

PREPARE cake mix as directed on package. Pour batter into greased 13×9-inch baking pan. Pour water and milk into large bowl. Add pudding mixes, sugar and cinnamon. Beat with electric mixer on low speed 1 to 2 minutes or until well blended. Pour over cake batter in pan.

BAKE 1 hour or until cake tester inserted in center comes out clean. Garnish as desired. Serve warm. *Makes 15 servings*

Preparation Time: 30 minutes
Baking Time: 1 hour

Fat Free Vanilla Sauce

> 3 cups cold skim milk
> 1 package (4-serving size) JELL-O Vanilla Flavor Fat Free Sugar Free Instant Reduced Calorie Pudding & Pie Filling
> ¼ teaspoon ground cinnamon (optional)

POUR milk into medium bowl. Add pudding mix and cinnamon. Beat with wire whisk 2 minutes. Cover.

REFRIGERATE until ready to serve. *Makes 3 cups*

 Nutrition Information Per Serving (2 tablespoons): 15 calories, 0g fat, 0mg cholesterol, 70mg sodium, 3g carbohydrate, 0g dietary fiber, 2g sugars, 1g protein

Preparation Time: 5 minutes

Saucy Bake

Gaiety Pastel Cookies

These fun fruit-flavored cookies were first developed in 1970. Sprinkling the tops with additional gelatin of the same flavor intensifies the color of the baked cookies.

In strawberry pink, lime green or berry blue, these cookies are sure to be a real hit.

3½ cups flour
 1 teaspoon CALUMET Baking Powder
1½ cups (3 sticks) butter or margarine
 1 cup sugar
 1 package (4-serving size) JELL-O Brand Gelatin Dessert, any flavor*
 1 egg
 1 teaspoon vanilla
 Additional JELL-O Brand Gelatin Dessert, any flavor*

HEAT oven to 400°F.

MIX flour and baking powder in medium bowl. Beat butter in large bowl with electric mixer to soften. Gradually add sugar and 1 package gelatin, beating until light and fluffy. Beat in egg and vanilla. Gradually add flour mixture, beating well after each addition.

SHAPE dough into 1-inch balls. Place on ungreased cookie sheets. Flatten with bottom of glass. Sprinkle with additional gelatin.

BAKE 10 to 12 minutes or until edges are lightly browned. Remove from cookie sheets. Cool on wire racks. Store in tightly covered container.   *Makes about 5 dozen*

*For best results, use same flavor.

Preparation Time: 40 minutes
Baking Time: 12 minutes

*Every eight seconds a box of JELL-O brand gelatin
is sold in the United States.*

Gaiety Pastel Cookies

Under-the-Sea Salad

Delightfully tangy with a hint of cinnamon.

This recipe dates back to the 1930's when automatic refrigerators arrived on the scene and lime flavor JELL-O gelatin was introduced for salads. Gelatin salads were easier and quicker to make than ever before and became very popular.

- 1 can (16 ounces) pear halves in syrup, undrained
- 1 cup boiling water
- 1 package (4-serving size) JELL-O Brand Lime Flavor Gelatin Dessert
- ¼ teaspoon salt (optional)
- 1 tablespoon lemon juice
- 2 packages (3 ounces each) PHILADELPHIA BRAND Cream Cheese, softened
- ⅛ teaspoon ground cinnamon (optional)

DRAIN pears, reserving ¾ cup of the syrup. Dice pears; set aside.

STIR boiling water into gelatin and salt in medium bowl at least 2 minutes until completely dissolved. Stir in reserved syrup and lemon juice. Pour 1¼ cups gelatin into 4-cup mold or 8×4-inch loaf pan. Refrigerate about 1 hour or until set but not firm (gelatin should stick to finger when touched and should mound).

MEANWHILE, stir remaining gelatin gradually into cream cheese in large bowl with wire whisk until smooth. Stir in pears and cinnamon. Spoon over gelatin layer in mold.

REFRIGERATE 4 hours or until firm. Unmold. Garnish as desired.

Makes 6 servings

Preparation Time: 20 minutes
Refrigerating Time: 5 hours

JELL-O®
Fun Facts

A JELL-O cartoon ad contest in 1921 challenged people to write or design a JELL-O ad. The $200 first prize was awarded based on "intelligence, composition, neatness, originality and availability." The winning ad and a photo of the creator were published four months later. The prize money was used to buy a horse.

*L*ow Fat Watergate Salad
(*Low Fat Pistachio Pineapple Delight*)

1 package (4-serving size) JELL-O Pistachio Flavor Fat Free Sugar Free Instant
    Reduced Calorie Pudding & Pie Filling
1 can (8 ounces) crushed pineapple in juice, undrained
1 container (8 ounces) BREYERS Vanilla Lowfat Yogurt
2 cups plus 6 tablespoons thawed COOL WHIP FREE Whipped Topping

STIR pudding mix, pineapple with juice and yogurt in large bowl until well blended.
Gently stir in 2 cups of the whipped topping.

REFRIGERATE 1 hour until ready to serve. Top each serving with 1 tablespoon of the
remaining whipped topping. *Makes 6 servings*

Nutrition Information Per Serving: 130 calories, 2g fat, less than 5mg cholesterol,
220mg sodium, 26g carbohydrate, 0g dietary fiber, 16g sugars, 2g protein

Preparation Time: 10 minutes
Refrigerating Time: 1 hour

This 1996 version of Watergate Salad, made with low fat yogurt and COOL WHIP FREE Whipped Topping, fits right in with today's healthier lifestyles.

*D*ouble Chocolate Bread Pudding

The queen of comfort foods!

5 cups milk
2 packages (4-serving size) JELL-O Chocolate Fudge Flavor Cook & Serve
    Pudding & Pie Filling (*not Instant*)
5 cups cubed French bread
1 cup BAKER'S Semi-Sweet Real Chocolate Chips

HEAT oven to 350°F.

POUR milk into large bowl. Add pudding mixes. Beat with wire whisk 1 minute.
Stir in bread. Pour pudding mixture into 13×9-inch baking dish. Sprinkle evenly
with chocolate chips.

BAKE 45 minutes or until mixture comes to boil. Remove from oven. Let stand
10 minutes. Serve warm. *Makes 15 servings*

Preparation Time: 15 minutes
Baking Time: 45 minutes

Chocolate is America's favorite flavor, so this warm fudgy chocolate pudding with added chocolate chips has twice the appeal.

Southern Banana Pudding

This layered pudding with a meringue topping was developed in 1949 from a recipe submitted by a consumer from Tennessee.

A classic expression of Southern hospitality.

1 package (4-serving size) JELL-O Vanilla or Banana Cream Flavor Cook & Serve Pudding & Pie Filling (*not Instant*)
2½ cups milk
2 egg yolks, well beaten
30 to 35 vanilla wafers
2 large bananas, sliced
2 egg whites
Dash salt
¼ cup sugar

HEAT oven to 350°F.

STIR pudding mix into milk in medium saucepan. Add egg yolks. Stirring constantly, cook on medium heat until mixture comes to full boil. Remove from heat.

ARRANGE layer of cookies on bottom and up side of 1½-quart baking dish. Add layer of banana slices; top with ⅓ of the pudding. Repeat layers twice, ending with pudding.

BEAT egg whites and salt in medium bowl with electric mixer on high speed until foamy. Gradually add sugar, beating until stiff peaks form. Spoon meringue mixture lightly onto pudding, spreading to edge of dish to seal.

BAKE 10 to 15 minutes or until meringue is lightly browned. Serve warm or refrigerate until ready to serve. *Makes 8 servings*

Preparation Time: 30 minutes
Baking Time: 15 minutes

" Look Jane, Jerry brought it! "

JELL-O®

America's most famous dessert

1924

89

Southern Banana Pudding

Creamy Vanilla Sauce

Developed in 1981 for a JELL-O Instant Pudding advertisement, variations on this sauce made with other pudding flavors have topped many a dessert.

An elegant topping for fresh fruit or gingerbread.

3½ cups cold milk, light cream or half-and-half
1 package (4-serving size) JELL-O Vanilla or French Vanilla Flavor Instant Pudding & Pie Filling

POUR milk into bowl. Add pudding mix. Beat with wire whisk 2 minutes. Cover.

REFRIGERATE until ready to serve. Serve over your favorite fruits or cake. Garnish as desired. *Makes 3½ cups*

Creamy Citrus Sauce: Add 2 teaspoons grated orange peel with pudding mix.

Preparation Time: 5 minutes

Gelatin Poke Cake

Perhaps the most successful JELL-O gelatin cake recipe, Gelatin Poke Cake can be made as cupcakes, a layer cake or this convenient sheet cake.

This fun cake can be made with any one of the 22 JELL-O gelatin flavors.

1 package (2-layer size) white cake mix or cake mix with pudding in the mix
1 cup boiling water
1 package (4-serving size) JELL-O Brand Gelatin Dessert, any flavor
½ cup cold water
1 tub (8 ounces) COOL WHIP Whipped Topping, thawed

HEAT oven to 350°F.

PREPARE and bake cake mix as directed on package for 13×9-inch baking pan. Remove from oven. Cool cake in pan 15 minutes. Pierce cake with large fork at ½-inch intervals.

MEANWHILE, stir boiling water into gelatin in medium bowl at least 2 minutes until completely dissolved. Stir in cold water; carefully pour over cake. Refrigerate 3 hours.

FROST with whipped topping. Refrigerate at least 1 hour or until ready to serve. Decorate as desired. *Makes 15 servings*

Preparation Time: 15 minutes
Baking Time: 35 minutes
Refrigerating Time: 4 hours

Creamy Vanilla Sauce

Vanilla Rice Pudding

Comfort food at its best—quick and easy, too.

Created in 1959 for a MINUTE Rice advertisement, Vanilla Rice Pudding combined two early convenience products to make a favorite traditional family dessert.

1 package (4-serving size) JELL-O Vanilla or Coconut Cream Flavor Cook & Serve Pudding & Pie Filling (*not Instant*)
4 cups milk
1 egg, well beaten
1 cup MINUTE Original Instant Enriched Rice, uncooked
¼ cup raisins (optional)
¼ teaspoon ground cinnamon*
⅛ teaspoon ground nutmeg*

STIR pudding mix into milk and egg in large saucepan. Stir in rice and raisins.

STIRRING constantly, cook on medium heat until mixture comes to full boil. Remove from heat. Cool 5 minutes, stirring twice.

POUR into dessert dishes or serving bowl. Serve warm or refrigerate until ready to serve. (For chilled pudding, place plastic wrap on surface of hot pudding. Refrigerate about 1 hour. Stir before serving.) Sprinkle with cinnamon and nutmeg. Garnish as desired.
Makes 8 servings

*Cinnamon and nutmeg can be added before cooking but pudding will be darker.

Note: *Recipe can be doubled.*

Preparation Time: 5 minutes
Cooking Time: 25 minutes

Better-Than-S_x Cake

Try it . . . you'll like it!

1½ **cups graham cracker crumbs**
⅔ **cup chopped pecans, divided**
½ **cup (1 stick) butter or margarine, melted**
6 **tablespoons sugar**
1 **package (8 ounces) PHILADELPHIA BRAND Cream Cheese, softened**
3½ **cups cold milk**
2 **packages (4-serving size) JELL-O Vanilla Flavor Instant Pudding & Pie Filling**
1⅓ **cups BAKER'S ANGEL FLAKE Coconut, divided**
1 **tub (8 ounces) COOL WHIP Whipped Topping, thawed**

This rich layered pudding dessert, created in 1980 as Layered Coconut Pecan Delight, just shows how times change but good taste doesn't!

MIX crumbs, ⅓ cup of the pecans, butter and sugar in 13×9-inch pan. Press firmly onto bottom of pan.

BEAT cream cheese in large bowl with electric mixer on low speed until smooth. Gradually beat in ½ cup of the milk. Add remaining milk and the pudding mixes. Beat on low speed about 2 minutes or until well blended. Stir in 1 cup of the coconut. Pour immediately over crust. Spread whipped topping evenly over the pudding mixture.

REFRIGERATE 2 hours or until set. Toast remaining ⅓ cup coconut and ⅓ cup pecans. Sprinkle over top of dessert. *Makes 15 servings*

Preparation Time: 30 minutes
Refrigerating Time: 2 hours

JELL-O®
Fun Facts

Children's fairy tales in JELL-O Land were the subject of a series of ads in the late 1920's. They featured the Sandman, the King, and a girl named Mary Jane. The situations encountered were all solved with delicious JELL-O recipes.

*S*triped Delight

This perennial favorite, combining cream cheese, whipped topping and instant pudding, was first made in 1983 and was originally called Cream Cheese Pudding Dessert.

A potluck favorite, this creamy dessert features a chocolatey pudding layer over a pecan shortbread crust.

> **1 cup flour**
> **1 cup finely chopped pecans**
> **¼ cup sugar (optional)**
> **½ cup (1 stick) butter or margarine, melted**
> **1 package (8 ounces) PHILADELPHIA BRAND Cream Cheese, softened**
> **¼ cup sugar**
> **2 tablespoons milk**
> **1 tub (8 ounces) COOL WHIP Whipped Topping, thawed**
> **3½ cups cold milk**
> **2 packages (4-serving size) JELL-O Chocolate Flavor Instant Pudding & Pie Filling**

HEAT oven to 350°F.

MIX flour, pecans and ¼ cup sugar in 13×9-inch baking pan. Stir in butter until flour is moistened. Press firmly onto bottom of pan. Bake 20 minutes or until lightly browned. Cool.

BEAT cream cheese, ¼ cup sugar and 2 tablespoons milk in large bowl with wire whisk until smooth. Gently stir in ½ of the whipped topping. Spread onto cooled crust.

POUR 3½ cups milk into large bowl. Add pudding mixes. Beat with wire whisk 1 to 2 minutes or until well blended. Pour over cream cheese layer.

REFRIGERATE 4 hours or until set. Just before serving, spread remaining whipped topping over pudding. Garnish as desired.   *Makes 15 servings*

Preparation Time: 30 minutes
Baking Time: 20 minutes
Refrigerating Time: 4 hours

Striped Delight

*R*ainbow Ribbon Mold

Gelatin recipes with layers of different flavors and textures date back to the early 1900's when they were called Neapolitans. They were often molded in loaf pans and served in slices to show the rainbow effect.

A real showpiece for a buffet or dinner party.

6¼ cups boiling water
5 packages (4-serving size) JELL-O Brand Gelatin Dessert, any 5 different flavors
1 cup (½ pint) BREAKSTONE'S Sour Cream or BREYERS Vanilla Lowfat Yogurt

STIR 1¼ cups boiling water into 1 flavor of gelatin in small bowl at least 2 minutes until completely dissolved. Pour ¾ cup of the dissolved gelatin into 6-cup ring mold. Refrigerate about 15 minutes until set but not firm (gelatin should stick to finger when touched and should mound). Refrigerate remaining gelatin in bowl about 5 minutes until slightly thickened (consistency of unbeaten egg whites). Gradually stir in 3 tablespoons of the sour cream. Spoon over gelatin in pan. Refrigerate about 15 minutes or until set but not firm (gelatin should stick to finger when touched and should mound).

MEANWHILE, repeat process with each remaining gelatin flavor. (Be sure to cool dissolved gelatin to room temperature before pouring into mold.) Refrigerate gelatin as directed to create a total of 10 alternating clear and creamy gelatin layers.

REFRIGERATE 2 hours or until firm. Unmold. Garnish as desired.

Makes 12 servings

Preparation Time: 1 hour
Refrigerating Time: 4½ hours

JELL-O gelatin is the largest-selling prepared dessert in America.

Rainbow Ribbon Mold

Apple Walnut Bread Pudding

A recipe for bread pudding appeared in an American cookbook as early as 1796. It has always been a favorite in the South and has re-emerged nationwide as a welcome "homey" dessert.

THE KING AND QUEEN MIGHT EAT THEREOF AND NOBLEMEN BESIDES

1921

Warm and fragrant, this is just the dessert for a chilly fall day.

4 cups cubed French bread
3 medium apples, chopped
1 cup chopped walnuts
4 cups milk
2 packages (4-serving size) JELL-O Vanilla Flavor Cook & Serve Pudding & Pie Filling (*not Instant*)
2 teaspoons ground cinnamon, divided

HEAT oven to 350°F.

PLACE bread cubes in lightly greased 13×9-inch baking dish. Add apples and walnuts; toss to mix well.

POUR milk into large bowl. Add pudding mixes and 1 teaspoon of the cinnamon. Beat with wire whisk 1 minute. Pour over bread mixture; sprinkle top with remaining cinnamon.

BAKE 50 to 60 minutes or until mixture comes to boil. Remove from oven. Let stand 10 minutes before serving. Serve warm.

Makes 15 servings

Preparation Time: 20 minutes
Baking Time: 1 hour

Dream Pie

This heavenly pie lives up to its name.

> **2 envelopes DREAM WHIP Whipped Topping Mix**
> **2¾ cups cold milk, divided**
> **1 teaspoon vanilla**
> **2 packages (4-serving size) JELL-O Instant Pudding & Pie Filling, any flavor**
> **1 baked pastry shell (9 inch), cooled, or 1 prepared graham cracker or chocolate flavor crumb crust (6 ounces)**

BEAT whipped topping mix, 1 cup of the milk and vanilla in large bowl with electric mixer on high speed 6 minutes or until topping thickens and forms peaks.

ADD remaining 1¾ cups milk and pudding mixes; beat on low speed until blended. Beat on high speed 2 minutes, scraping bowl occasionally. Spoon into pastry shell.

REFRIGERATE at least 4 hours.

Makes 8 servings

Preparation Time: 15 minutes
Refrigerating Time: 4 hours

During World War II, one-crust pies became popular because of the scarcity of shortening. Many were filled with JELL-O gelatin or pudding—convenient products for women involved in the war effort.

Mini Chocolate Tarts

Enjoy a touch of elegance with these silky smooth miniature desserts.

> **1 package (9.2 ounces) JELL-O No Bake Chocolate Silk Pie**
> **⅓ cup butter or margarine, melted**
> **1⅔ cups cold milk**

MIX crumbs and butter thoroughly with fork in small bowl until crumbs are well moistened. Press onto bottoms of 12 paper-lined muffin cups.

BEAT milk and filling mix with electric mixer on low speed until blended. Beat on medium speed 3 minutes. (Filling will be thick.) Spoon over crumb mixture in muffin cups.

REFRIGERATE at least 1 hour or until ready to serve.

Makes 12

Preparation Time: 15 minutes
Refrigerating Time: 1 hour

Chocolate Silk Pie, the second JELL-O No Bake Dessert, joined the line in 1984.

Watergate Salad (Pistachio Pineapple Delight)

Originally named Pistachio Pineapple Delight, Watergate Salad first surfaced in 1976, the year Pistachio Flavor Instant Pudding & Pie Filling was launched.

Serve as a salad with cold sliced cooked chicken or as dessert on its own.

> 1 package (4-serving size) JELL-O Pistachio Flavor Instant Pudding & Pie Filling
> 1 can (20 ounces) crushed pineapple in juice, undrained
> 1 cup miniature marshmallows
> ½ cup chopped nuts
> 2 cups thawed COOL WHIP Whipped Topping

STIR pudding mix, pineapple with juice, marshmallows and nuts in large bowl until well blended. Gently stir in whipped topping.

REFRIGERATE 1 hour or until ready to serve. Garnish as desired.

Makes 8 servings

Preparation Time: 10 minutes
Refrigerating Time: 1 hour

Fruity Vanilla Cream

The simple concept of combining JELL-O Gelatin with JELL-O Vanilla Instant Pudding produces a refreshingly creamy dessert the family will go for in a big way.

Serve a different flavor every night!

> 1 cup boiling water
> 1 package (4-serving size) JELL-O Brand Gelatin Dessert, any flavor
> ½ cup cold water
> 2 cups cold milk
> 1 package (4-serving size) JELL-O Vanilla Flavor Instant Pudding & Pie Filling

STIR boiling water into gelatin in medium bowl at least 2 minutes until completely dissolved. Stir in cold water. Refrigerate about 1 hour or until slightly thickened (consistency of unbeaten egg whites).

POUR milk into large bowl. Add pudding mix. Beat with wire whisk 1 minute. Beat in thickened gelatin. Pour into serving bowl or individual dishes.

REFRIGERATE 2 hours or until set.

Makes 6 servings

Preparation Time: 15 minutes
Refrigerating Time: 3 hours

101

Watergate Salad (Pistachio Pineapple Delight)

Luscious Pies

JELL-O brand gelatins and puddings make pies to die for—fruit pies, chiffon pies, glazed pies, layered pies, frozen pies, cream pies and cheesecake pies! If you are one who considers making pies too time-consuming, open your eyes to these. Most take 20 minutes or less to prepare, and none require advanced cooking skills.

In the 1940's when war-time rationing made shortening difficult to obtain, one-crust pies filled with gelatin and pudding mixtures became popular. Since then, prepared pie crusts have become available, further reducing pie-making time.

So pile on the pies . . . your family will love you for it!

Top to bottom: Glazed Fruit Pie (page 113), Cookies-and-Cream Ice Cream Shop Pie (page 107),
Strawberry Lime Pie (page 112), White Chocolate-Devil's Food Pie (page 106)

 Lemon Chiffon Pie

Cool, easy and incredibly delicious!

No need to separate eggs and beat the whites for this airy pie. Just follow these simple preparation steps.

⅔ **cup boiling water**
1 **package (4-serving size) JELL-O Brand Lemon Flavor Gelatin Dessert**
2 **teaspoons grated lemon peel**
2 **tablespoons lemon juice**
½ **cup cold water**
   Ice cubes
1 **tub (8 ounces) COOL WHIP Whipped Topping, thawed**
1 **prepared graham cracker crumb crust (6 ounces)**

STIR boiling water into gelatin in large bowl at least 2 minutes until completely dissolved. Stir in lemon peel and juice. Mix cold water and ice to make 1¼ cups. Add to gelatin, stirring until slightly thickened. Remove any remaining ice.

STIR in whipped topping with wire whisk until smooth. Refrigerate 20 to 30 minutes or until mixture is very thick and will mound. Spoon into crust.

REFRIGERATE 6 hours or overnight until firm. Garnish as desired.

Makes 8 servings

Preparation Time: 20 minutes
Refrigerating Time: 6½ hours

105

Lemon Chiffon Pie

White Chocolate-Devil's Food Pie

JELL-O Fat Free Instant Pudding & Pie Filling, specially formulated to work with skim milk, was introduced in 1994 for those seeking ways to reduce fat in their diets.

Creamy dark and white chocolate pudding layers team together to make a scrumptious dessert.

> **2 cups cold skim milk, divided**
> **1 package (4-serving size) JELL-O Devil's Food Flavor Fat Free Instant Pudding & Pie Filling**
> **1 tub (8 ounces) COOL WHIP FREE or COOL WHIP LITE Whipped Topping, thawed**
> **1 prepared reduced fat graham cracker crumb crust (6 ounces)**
> **1 package (4-serving size) JELL-O White Chocolate Flavor Fat Free Instant Pudding & Pie Filling**

POUR 1 cup of the milk into medium bowl. Add devil's food flavor pudding mix. Beat with wire whisk 1 minute. (Mixture will be thick.) Gently stir in ½ of the whipped topping. Spoon evenly into crust.

POUR remaining 1 cup milk into another medium bowl. Add white chocolate flavor pudding mix. Beat with wire whisk 1 minute. (Mixture will be thick.) Gently stir in remaining whipped topping. Spread over pudding layer in crust.

REFRIGERATE 4 hours or until set. Garnish as desired.   *Makes 8 servings*

 Nutrition Information Per Serving (using COOL WHIP FREE and omitting garnish): *270 calories, 5g fat, 0mg cholesterol, 490mg sodium, 53g carbohydrate, less than 1g dietary fiber, 4g protein, 10% daily value calcium*

Preparation Time: 10 minutes
Refrigerating Time: 4 hours

Ice Cream Shop Pie

Favorite ice cream flavors in a quick-to-make pie.

1½ cups cold milk, half-and-half or light cream
1 package (4-serving size) JELL-O Instant
    Pudding & Pie Filling
1 tub (8 ounces) COOL WHIP Whipped
    Topping, thawed
1 prepared crumb crust (6 ounces)

POUR milk into large bowl. Add pudding mix. Beat with wire whisk 2 minutes. Gently stir in whipped topping. Spoon into crust.

FREEZE 6 hours or overnight until firm. Let stand at room temperature or in refrigerator 15 minutes or until pie can be cut easily.

GARNISH as desired.   *Makes 8 servings*

Cookies-and-Cream Pie: Use JELL-O Vanilla Flavor Instant Pudding & Pie Filling and chocolate crumb crust. Stir in 1 cup chopped chocolate sandwich cookies with whipped topping.

Rocky Road Pie: Use JELL-O Chocolate Flavor Instant Pudding & Pie Filling and chocolate crumb crust. Stir in ⅓ cup each BAKER'S Semi-Sweet Real Chocolate Chips, miniature marshmallows and chopped nuts with whipped topping. Serve with chocolate sauce, if desired.

Peanut Butter Pie: Use JELL-O Vanilla Flavor Instant Pudding & Pie Filling and graham cracker crumb crust. Reduce milk to 1 cup and add ½ cup peanut butter with pudding mix. Serve with chocolate sauce and chopped peanuts, if desired.

Preparation Time: 15 minutes
Freezing Time: 6 hours

Instant pudding & pie filling and whipped topping provide the base for these delectable freezer pies with a variety of stir-in ingredients.

1938

107

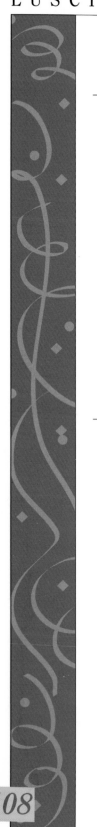

Creamy Chocolate Pie

This will delight family and guests alike.

Preparation time for this luscious pie takes only 10 minutes.

1¾ cups cold milk
2 packages (4-serving size) JELL-O Chocolate or Chocolate Fudge Flavor
  Instant Pudding & Pie Filling
1 tub (8 ounces) COOL WHIP Whipped Topping, thawed
1 prepared chocolate flavor crumb crust (6 ounces)

POUR milk into large bowl. Add pudding mixes. Beat with wire whisk until well mixed. (Mixture will be thick.) Immediately stir in whipped topping. Spoon into crust.

REFRIGERATE 4 hours or until set. Garnish as desired.   *Makes 8 servings*

Preparation Time: 10 minutes
Refrigerating Time: 4 hours

Frozen Cheesecake Pie

This frosty cheesecake dessert features a fruity cherry swirl filling.

Most JELL-O No Bake desserts include crust, filling and topping for great-looking, great-tasting desserts that are easy to prepare.

1 package (21.4 ounces) JELL-O No Bake Cherry or Strawberry
  Topped Cheesecake
2 tablespoons sugar
⅓ cup butter or margarine, melted
1½ cups cold milk
1 tub (8 ounces) COOL WHIP Whipped Topping, thawed

MIX crumbs, sugar and butter thoroughly with fork in 9-inch pie plate until crumbs are well moistened. Press firmly against side of plate first, using finger or large spoon to shape edge. Press remaining crumbs firmly onto bottom using measuring cup.

BEAT milk and filling mix in medium bowl with electric mixer on low speed until blended. Beat on medium speed 3 minutes. (Filling will be thick.) Stir in whipped topping until smooth. Swirl fruit topping into mixture with spatula. Spoon into crust.

FREEZE 6 hours or overnight until firm. Let stand at room temperature or in refrigerator 15 minutes or until pie can be cut easily.   *Makes 8 servings*

Preparation Time: 15 minutes
Freezing Time: 6 hours

Creamy Chocolate Pie

COOL 'N EASY® Pie

This pie, which is a mixture of gelatin and whipped topping, was first created in 1978. It offers many variations featuring different JELL-O flavors and fresh fruit combinations.

America's most famous dessert

JELL-O

1925

Ten minutes in the morning—luscious strawberry pie in the evening!

⅔ cup boiling water
1 package (4-serving size) JELL-O Brand Gelatin Dessert, any red flavor
½ cup cold water
   Ice cubes
1 tub (8 ounces) COOL WHIP Whipped Topping, thawed
1 cup chopped strawberries
1 prepared graham cracker crumb crust (6 ounces)

STIR boiling water into gelatin in large bowl at least 2 minutes until completely dissolved. Mix cold water and ice to make 1¼ cups. Add to gelatin, stirring until slightly thickened. Remove any remaining ice.

STIR in whipped topping with wire whisk until smooth. Mix in strawberries. Refrigerate 20 to 30 minutes or until mixture is very thick and will mound. Spoon into crust.

REFRIGERATE 6 hours or overnight until firm. Garnish as desired. *Makes 8 servings*

Preparation Time: 10 minutes
Refrigerating Time: 6½ hours

COOL 'N EASY® Pie

Strawberry Lime Pie

The JELL-O brand has always kept up with the times— dessert ideas that fit the demands of contemporary lifestyles.

This fluffy concoction beautifully complements the tartness of fresh berries.

⅔ **cup boiling water**
1 **package (4-serving size) JELL-O Brand Lime Flavor Gelatin Dessert**
½ **teaspoon grated lime peel**
2 **tablespoons lime juice**
½ **cup cold water**
  Ice cubes
1 **tub (8 ounces) COOL WHIP Whipped Topping, thawed**
1 **cup sliced strawberries**
1 **prepared graham cracker crumb crust (6 ounces)**

STIR boiling water into gelatin in large bowl at least 2 minutes until completely dissolved. Stir in lime peel and juice. Mix cold water and ice to make 1 cup. Add to gelatin, stirring until slightly thickened. Remove any remaining ice.

STIR in 2½ cups of the whipped topping with wire whisk until smooth. Gently stir in strawberries. Refrigerate 30 minutes or until mixture is very thick and will mound. Spoon into crust.

REFRIGERATE 4 hours or until firm. Top with remaining whipped topping. Garnish as desired.   *Makes 8 servings*

Preparation Time: 20 minutes
Refrigerating Time: 4½ hours

In 1943, a JELL-O ad featured singer Kate Smith with a wartime message on managing scarce and rationed foods: "We can be careful to buy and cook only what we need! And we can think up smart ways to use leftovers."

Glazed Fruit Pie

Try different fruits and JELL-O pudding flavors to create variations of this fabulous pie.

1½ **cups cold milk or half-and-half**
  1 **package (4-serving size) JELL-O Vanilla Flavor Instant Pudding & Pie Filling**
  1 **prepared graham cracker crumb crust (6 ounces) or 1 baked pastry shell**
    (9 inch), cooled
  1 **cup boiling water**
  1 **package (4-serving size) JELL-O Brand Lemon, Peach or Orange Flavor Gelatin**
    Dessert, or any red flavor
  ½ **cup cold water**
1½ **cups fresh or drained canned fruit***

POUR milk into large bowl. Add pudding mix. Beat with wire whisk 1 minute. Pour into crust. Refrigerate 1 hour.

STIR boiling water into gelatin in large bowl at least 2 minutes until completely dissolved. Stir in cold water. Refrigerate 1 hour or until thickened (spoon drawn through leaves definite impression). Pour 1 cup gelatin over the pudding layer. Arrange fruit on gelatin. Spoon remaining gelatin over fruit.

REFRIGERATE 2 hours or until firm.   *Makes 8 servings*

*Use any variety of berries, mandarin orange sections, sliced bananas, peaches or plums, or halved seedless grapes.

Preparation Time: 15 minutes
Refrigerating Time: 4 hours

This creamy pie, topped with fruit encased in clear gelatin, was first featured in a 1985 television commercial for JELL-O brand pudding.

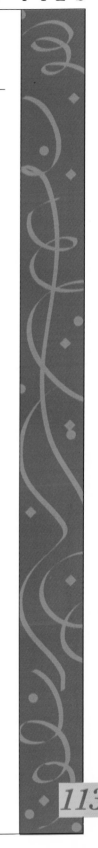

113

Frozen Banana Split Pie

The family will go nuts over this ice cream parlor dessert!

JELL-O pudding with whipped topping stirred in freezes beautifully to produce a smooth-textured frozen dessert.

1½ **bananas, sliced**
1 **prepared graham cracker crumb crust (6 ounces)**
2 **cups cold milk**
1 **package (4-serving size) JELL-O Vanilla or Banana Cream Flavor Instant Pudding & Pie Filling**
1 **tub (8 ounces) COOL WHIP Whipped Topping, thawed**
 Chocolate, strawberry and pineapple dessert toppings
 Additional banana slices
 Chopped nuts

ARRANGE banana slices on bottom of crust; set aside.

POUR milk into large bowl. Add pudding mix. Beat with wire whisk 1 minute. Gently stir in 2 cups of the whipped topping. Spread over banana slices.

FREEZE 6 hours or until firm. Let stand at room temperature or in refrigerator 15 minutes or until pie can be cut easily. Top with dessert toppings, remaining whipped topping, banana slices and nuts. *Makes 8 servings*

Preparation Time: 15 minutes
Freezing Time: 6 hours

Pastel Party Pie

Nothing could be simpler . . . or taste better!

Originally called Ice Cream Parfait Pie, this gelatin-ice cream pie was first created in 1952 and has adapted well to the many new flavors of JELL-O gelatin.

1¼ **cups boiling water**
1 **package (4-serving size) JELL-O Brand Gelatin Dessert, any flavor**
1 **pint (2 cups) ice cream (any flavor), softened**
1 **prepared graham cracker crumb crust (6 ounces)**

STIR boiling water into gelatin in large bowl at least 2 minutes until completely dissolved. Stir in ice cream until melted and smooth. Refrigerate 15 to 20 minutes or until mixture is very thick and will mound. Spoon into crust.

REFRIGERATE 2 hours or until firm. *Makes 8 servings*

Preparation Time: 10 minutes
Refrigerating Time: 2½ hours

115

Frozen Banana Split Pie

Chocolate Mallow Cookie Pie

An American family favorite for nearly 70 years, JELL-O Pudding & Instant Pie Filling is now available in 51 flavors.

This will be a big hit with the family!

> **2 cups miniature marshmallows**
> **2 tablespoons milk**
> **2½ cups thawed COOL WHIP Whipped Topping**
> **2 cups cold milk**
> **2 packages (4-serving size) JELL-O Chocolate Flavor Instant Pudding & Pie Filling**
> **1 prepared chocolate flavor crumb crust (6 ounces)**
> **14 vanilla wafers**
> **Chocolate Topping (recipe follows, optional)**

MICROWAVE marshmallows and 2 tablespoons milk in medium microwavable bowl on HIGH 1 minute, stirring after 30 seconds. Stir until marshmallows are melted. Refrigerate 15 minutes to cool. Gently stir in 1 cup of the whipped topping.

POUR 2 cups milk into large bowl. Add pudding mixes. Beat with wire whisk just until mixed. Immediately stir in remaining whipped topping.

SPOON pudding mixture into crust. Arrange cookies on top. Spread marshmallow mixture over cookies. Drizzle with Chocolate Topping, if desired.

REFRIGERATE 4 hours or until set.   *Makes 8 servings*

Chocolate Topping: Microwave 2 squares BAKER'S Semi-Sweet Baking Chocolate in heavy zipper-style plastic sandwich bag on HIGH 1 to 2 minutes or until chocolate is almost melted. Add 2 teaspoons softened butter; gently squeeze bag until chocolate and butter are completely melted. Fold down top of bag; snip tiny piece off 1 corner from bottom of bag to drizzle chocolate.

Preparation Time: 30 minutes
Refrigerating Time: 4¼ hours

Chocolate Mallow Cookie Pie

Strawberry Fruited Pie

JELL-O sugar free gelatin was introduced in 1982 and marketed nationally in 1984 to fit contemporary eating styles.

1½ cups boiling water
1 package (8-serving size) or 2 packages (4-serving size) JELL-O Brand Strawberry Flavor Sugar Free Low Calorie Gelatin Dessert or JELL-O Brand Strawberry Flavor Gelatin Dessert
1 cup ice cubes
2 pints strawberries, sliced
1 whole graham cracker, crushed

SPRAY 9-inch pie plate lightly with no stick cooking spray.

STIR boiling water into gelatin in large bowl at least 2 minutes until completely dissolved. Add ice cubes, stirring until completely melted. Refrigerate 30 minutes or until slightly thickened (consistency of unbeaten egg whites).

STIR in strawberries. Pour into pie plate. Sprinkle graham cracker crumbs around edge of pie.

REFRIGERATE 4 hours or until firm.   *Makes 8 servings*

 Nutrition Information Per Serving (using JELL-O Brand Strawberry Flavor Sugar Free Low Calorie Gelatin Dessert): *40 calories, 0g fat, 0mg cholesterol, 70mg sodium, 7g carbohydrate, 2g dietary fiber, 5g sugars, 2g protein, 80% daily value vitamin C*

Preparation Time: 15 minutes
Refrigerating Time: 4½ hours

In the late 1930's, the phrase "Look for the Big Red Letters on the Box" made its appearance in comic strip-type ads featuring Jack Benny and Mary Livingston.

Ice Cream Pudding Pie

1 cup cold milk
1 cup ice cream (any flavor), softened
1 package (4-serving size) JELL-O Instant Pudding & Pie Filling, any flavor
1 prepared graham cracker crumb crust (6 ounces)

MIX milk and ice cream in large bowl. Add pudding mix. Beat with electric mixer on lowest speed 1 minute. Pour immediately into crust.

REFRIGERATE 2 hours or until set.

Makes 8 servings

Preparation Time: 10 minutes
Refrigerating Time: 2 hours

Developed in 1957, this recipe has many variations. Try vanilla pudding with coffee, pistachio or vanilla ice cream; or chocolate pudding with vanilla, peppermint or coffee ice cream.

Caramel Chocolate Pie

¼ cup KRAFT Caramel or Butterscotch Flavored Dessert Topping
1 prepared chocolate flavor or graham cracker crumb crust (6 ounces)
½ cup chopped pecans
3 cups cold milk
2 packages (4-serving size) JELL-O Chocolate Flavor Instant Pudding & Pie Filling
Thawed COOL WHIP Whipped Topping

SPREAD caramel topping onto bottom of crust. Sprinkle with pecans.

POUR milk into large bowl. Add pudding mixes. Beat with wire whisk 1 minute. Pour immediately into crust.

REFRIGERATE 4 hours or until set. Top with whipped topping.   *Makes 8 servings*

Preparation Time: 15 minutes
Refrigerating Time: 4 hours

Key Lime Pie

Key Lime Pie is typically made with small tart limes grown in Florida, not generally available in the rest of the U.S. This is a quick, easy adaptation.

Taste this cool summertime treat.

1¾ cups boiling water
1 package (8-serving size) or 2 packages (4-serving size) JELL-O Brand Lime Flavor Gelatin Dessert
2 teaspoons grated lime peel
¼ cup lime juice
1 pint (2 cups) vanilla ice cream, softened
1 prepared graham cracker crumb crust (6 ounces)

STIR boiling water into gelatin in large bowl at least 2 minutes until completely dissolved. Stir in lime peel and juice.

STIR in ice cream until melted and smooth. Refrigerate 15 to 20 minutes or until mixture is very thick and will mound. Spoon into crust.

REFRIGERATE 2 hours or until firm. Garnish as desired.   *Makes 8 servings*

Preparation Time: 15 minutes
Refrigerating Time: 2½ hours

Raspberry Yogurt Pie

The red JELL-O flavors—strawberry, cherry and raspberry—are the most popular, followed by orange and lime.

⅔ cup boiling water
1 package (4-serving size) JELL-O Brand Raspberry Flavor Gelatin Dessert
1 cup vanilla frozen lowfat yogurt, softened
2 cups thawed COOL WHIP Whipped Topping
1 cup raspberries
1 prepared chocolate flavor crumb crust (6 ounces)

STIR boiling water into gelatin in large bowl at least 2 minutes until completely dissolved. Stir in frozen yogurt until melted and smooth.

STIR in whipped topping and raspberries. Refrigerate 15 minutes or until mixture is very thick and will mound. Spoon into crust.

REFRIGERATE 2 hours or until firm.   *Makes 8 servings*

Preparation Time: 20 minutes
Refrigerating Time: 2¼ hours

121

Key Lime Pie

Summer Berry Pie

Strawberry is, hands down, the most popular flavor of JELL-O and has been for 100 years.

Pure joy is this fresh berry pie!

¾ **cup sugar**
3 **tablespoons cornstarch**
1½ **cups water**
1 **package (4-serving size) JELL-O Brand Gelatin Dessert, any red flavor**
1 **cup blueberries**
1 **cup raspberries**
1 **cup sliced strawberries**
1 **prepared graham cracker crumb crust (6 ounces)**
2 **cups thawed COOL WHIP Whipped Topping**

MIX sugar and cornstarch in medium saucepan. Gradually stir in water until smooth. Stirring constantly, cook on medium heat until mixture comes to boil; boil 1 minute. Remove from heat. Stir in gelatin until completely dissolved. Cool to room temperature. Stir in berries. Pour into crust.

REFRIGERATE 3 hours or until firm. Top with whipped topping.

Makes 8 servings

Preparation Time: 20 minutes
Refrigerating Time: 3 hours

Every day more than 820,000 packages of JELL-O are purchased or prepared and eaten.

123

Summer Berry Pie

Chocolate Banana Pudding Pie

JELL-O pudding is in nearly half of the households in America.

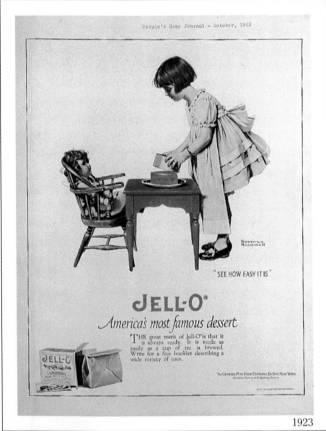

1923

A real treat made extra special with a luscious chocolate-coated graham cracker crust.

4 squares BAKER'S Semi-Sweet Baking Chocolate
2 tablespoons milk
1 tablespoon butter or margarine
1 prepared graham cracker crumb crust (6 ounces)
1½ to 2 medium bananas, sliced
2¾ cups cold milk
2 packages (4-serving size) JELL-O Vanilla or Banana Flavor Instant Pudding & Pie Filling

MICROWAVE chocolate, 2 tablespoons milk and butter in medium microwavable bowl on HIGH 1 to 1½ minutes, stirring every 30 seconds. Stir until chocolate is completely melted. Spread evenly onto bottom of crust. Refrigerate 30 minutes or until chocolate is firm. Arrange banana slices over chocolate.

POUR 2¾ cups milk into large bowl. Add pudding mixes. Beat with wire whisk 1 minute. Spread over banana slices.

REFRIGERATE 4 hours or until set.

Makes 8 servings

Preparation Time: 20 minutes
Refrigerating Time: 4½ hours

124

*P*ineapple Coconut Pie

Enjoy tropical piña colada flavors in a new form.

⅔ **cup boiling water**
1 **package (4-serving size) JELL-O Brand Island Pineapple or Orange Flavor Gelatin Dessert**
¼ **cup rum***
½ **cup cold water**
  Ice cubes
1 **tub (8 ounces) COOL WHIP Whipped Topping, thawed**
1 **can (8 ounces) crushed pineapple in juice, drained**
½ **cup BAKER'S ANGEL FLAKE Coconut**
1 **prepared graham cracker crumb crust (6 ounces)**
  Toasted BAKER'S ANGEL FLAKE Coconut (optional)

Piña colada, which means "strained pineapple" in Spanish, refers to a tropical island drink with coconut cream, pineapple juice and rum.

STIR boiling water into gelatin in large bowl at least 2 minutes until completely dissolved. Stir in rum. Mix cold water and ice to make 1¼ cups. Add to gelatin, stirring until slightly thickened. Remove any remaining ice.

STIR in whipped topping using wire whisk until smooth. Gently stir in pineapple and coconut. Refrigerate 20 to 30 minutes or until mixture is very thick and will mound. Spoon into crust.

REFRIGERATE 4 hours or until firm. Sprinkle with toasted coconut, if desired.

Makes 8 servings

*Or use 1½ teaspoons rum extract.

Preparation Time: 20 minutes
Refrigerating Time: 4½ hours

125

Double Layer Chocolate Pie

To quickly soften cream cheese, microwave on HIGH for 15 to 20 seconds.

4 ounces PHILADELPHIA BRAND Cream Cheese, softened
1 tablespoon milk or half-and-half
1 tablespoon sugar
1 tub (8 ounces) COOL WHIP Whipped Topping, thawed
1 prepared chocolate flavor crumb crust (6 ounces)
2 cups cold milk or half-and-half
2 packages (4-serving size) JELL-O Chocolate Flavor Instant Pudding & Pie Filling

MIX cream cheese, 1 tablespoon milk and sugar in large bowl with wire whisk until smooth. Gently stir in 1½ cups of the whipped topping. Spread onto bottom of crust.

POUR 2 cups milk into bowl. Add pudding mixes. Beat with wire whisk until well mixed. (Mixture will be thick.) Immediately stir in remaining whipped topping. Spread over cream cheese layer.

REFRIGERATE 4 hours or until set. Garnish as desired.   *Makes 8 servings*

Preparation Time: 15 minutes
Refrigerating Time: 4 hours

Rocky Road Chocolate Silk Pie

JELL-O No Bake desserts, containing JELL-O pudding, were created for busy households with children. They take about 15 minutes to prepare and are ready to serve in an hour.

1 package (9.2 ounces) JELL-O No Bake Chocolate Silk Pie
⅓ cup butter or margarine, melted
1⅔ cups cold milk
1 cup miniature marshmallows
½ cup chopped nuts

MIX crumbs and butter thoroughly with fork in 9-inch pie plate until crumbs are well moistened. Press firmly against side of pie plate first, using finger or large spoon to shape edge. Press remaining crumbs firmly onto bottom using measuring cup.

BEAT milk and filling mix with electric mixer on low speed until blended. Beat on medium speed 3 minutes. (Filling will be thick.) Stir in marshmallows and nuts. Spoon into crust.

REFRIGERATE at least 1 hour.   *Makes 8 servings*

Preparation Time: 15 minutes
Refrigerating Time: 1 hour

127

Double Layer Chocolate Pie

Sensational Desserts

Choose from cakes, terrines, cheesecakes, bars and layered desserts with a wide variety of presentations—some are marbled, others glazed, frosted or crowned with whipped topping and/or fruit.

They're beautiful, easy and delicious. When you plan to feed eight to fifteen, these are just the desserts you need. What more can you ask? Many are made in 13×9-inch pans, so they're perfect to carry to a backyard or potluck gathering.

*Top to bottom: Strawberry Lime Dessert (page 133), Orange Pineapple Layered Dessert (page 132),
Layered Chocolate Cheesecake Squares (page 141), Pudding Poke Cake (page 154)*

White Chocolate Cheesecake

Take the mystery out of making cheesecakes with this recipe made extra simple with JELL-O No Bake Cheesecake.

A truly luxurious dessert with a rich, silky texture.

- 1 package (11.1 ounces) JELL-O No Bake Real Cheesecake
- 2 tablespoons sugar
- ⅓ cup butter or margarine, melted
- 1½ cups cold milk
- 1 package (6 squares) BAKER'S Premium White Baking Chocolate Squares, melted
- 2 squares BAKER'S Semi-Sweet Baking Chocolate, melted (optional)

MIX crumbs, sugar and butter thoroughly with fork in 9-inch pie plate until crumbs are well moistened. Press firmly against side of pie plate first, using finger or large spoon to shape edge. Press remaining crumbs firmly onto bottom using measuring cup.

BEAT milk and filling mix with electric mixer on low speed until blended. Beat on medium speed 3 minutes. (Filling will be thick.) Reserve about 3 tablespoons melted white chocolate for garnish, if desired. Stir remaining melted white chocolate into filling mixture. Spoon into crust. Drizzle with reserved melted white chocolate and melted semi-sweet chocolate, if desired.

REFRIGERATE at least 1 hour.

Makes 8 servings

Preparation Time: 15 minutes
Refrigerating Time: 1 hour

1946

White Chocolate Cheesecake

Orange Pineapple Layered Dessert

Some fruits sink and others float when added to JELL-O. Sinkers include mandarin oranges, seedless grapes, and drained slices or chunks of canned fruits. Floaters are slices of banana, apple, strawberries, fresh peaches and pears, and fresh orange sections.

Even the kids will love this tasty dessert perfect for family gatherings.

1½ cups boiling water
1 package (8-serving size) or 2 packages (4-serving size) JELL-O Brand Orange Flavor Gelatin Dessert
1 cup cold water
1 can (20 ounces) crushed pineapple in juice, undrained
1 can (11 ounces) mandarin orange segments, drained
1½ cups graham cracker crumbs
½ cup sugar, divided
½ cup (1 stick) butter or margarine, melted
1 package (8 ounces) PHILADELPHIA BRAND Cream Cheese, softened
2 tablespoons milk
1 tub (8 ounces) COOL WHIP Whipped Topping, thawed

STIR boiling water into gelatin in large bowl at least 2 minutes until completely dissolved. Stir in cold water, pineapple with juice and oranges. Refrigerate about 1¼ hours or until slightly thickened (consistency of unbeaten egg whites).

MIX crumbs, ¼ cup of the sugar and butter in 13×9-inch pan. Press firmly onto bottom of pan. Refrigerate until ready to fill.

BEAT cream cheese, remaining ¼ cup sugar and milk in large bowl until smooth. Gently stir in 2 cups of the whipped topping. Spread evenly over crust. Spoon gelatin over cream cheese layer.

REFRIGERATE 3 hours or until firm. Garnish with remaining whipped topping.

Makes 15 servings

Preparation Time: 30 minutes
Refrigerating Time: 4¼ hours

Strawberry Lime Dessert

A delicate crystal bowl will showcase this elegant fat free dessert in style.

2 cups boiling water
1 package (4-serving size) JELL-O Brand Lime Flavor Sugar Free Low Calorie
    Gelatin Dessert or JELL-O Brand Lime Flavor Gelatin Dessert
½ cup cold water
1 container (8 ounces) BREYERS Vanilla Lowfat Yogurt
1 package (4-serving size) JELL-O Brand Strawberry Flavor Sugar Free Low
    Calorie Gelatin Dessert or JELL-O Brand Strawberry Flavor Gelatin Dessert
1 package (10 ounces) frozen strawberries in lite syrup, unthawed

STIR 1 cup of the boiling water into lime gelatin in medium bowl at least 2 minutes until completely dissolved. Stir in cold water. Refrigerate about 45 minutes or until slightly thickened (consistency of unbeaten egg whites). Stir in yogurt with wire whisk until smooth. Pour into 2-quart serving bowl. Refrigerate about 15 minutes or until set but not firm (gelatin should stick to finger when touched and should mound).

STIR remaining 1 cup boiling water into strawberry gelatin in medium bowl at least 2 minutes until completely dissolved. Stir in frozen berries until berries are separated and gelatin is thickened (spoon drawn through leaves definite impression). Spoon over lime gelatin mixture.

REFRIGERATE 2 hours or until firm. Garnish as desired.   *Makes 10 servings*

Nutrition Information Per Serving (using JELL-O Brand Strawberry and Lime Flavors Sugar Free Low Calorie Gelatin Dessert and omitting garnish): *60 calories, 0g fat, less than 5mg cholesterol, 65mg sodium, 11g carbohydrate, less than 1g dietary fiber, 9g sugars, 2g protein, 15% daily value vitamin C*

Preparation Time: 15 minutes
Refrigerating Time: 3 hours

Fruits frequently used in early recipes were strawberries, peaches, pineapple, apricots, cherries, prunes, raisins, dates and bananas.

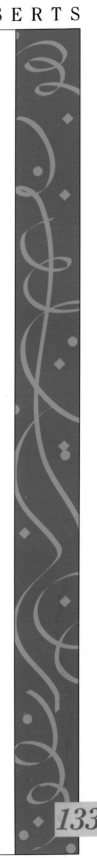

 Pinwheel Cake and Cream

Convenience and dependability have been key ingredients in JELL-O products from the start. With JELL-O Instant Pudding & Pie Filling on hand, dessert is only about 15 minutes away.

An easy and elegant dessert perfect for those last-minute guests.

2 cups cold milk
1 package (4-serving size) JELL-O Vanilla or French Vanilla Flavor Instant Pudding & Pie Filling
1 cup thawed COOL WHIP Whipped Topping
1 small peach or nectarine, chopped
1 teaspoon grated orange peel
1 package (12 ounces) pound cake, cut into slices
2 cups summer fruits, such as sliced peaches, nectarines or plums; seedless grapes; strawberries, raspberries or blueberries

POUR milk into large bowl. Add pudding mix. Beat with wire whisk 1 minute. Gently stir in whipped topping, chopped peach and grated peel.

ARRANGE pound cake slices on serving plate. Spoon pudding mixture evenly over cake. Top with fruits. Serve immediately or cover and refrigerate until ready to serve.

Makes 10 servings

Preparation Time: 15 minutes

135

Pinwheel Cake and Cream

Easy Eclair Dessert

In the late 1970's, JELL-O pudding was promoted for "Easy Homemade Desserts"—recipes which took little time and trouble, tasted delicious and used pudding as the basic building block.

A fabulous treat—perfect for a potluck party.

27 whole graham crackers
3 cups cold milk
2 packages (4-serving size) JELL-O Vanilla Flavor Instant Pudding & Pie Filling
1 tub (8 ounces) COOL WHIP Whipped Topping, thawed
1 can (16 ounces) chocolate fudge frosting

ARRANGE 9 of the crackers on bottom of 13×9-inch pan, cutting crackers to fit, if necessary.

POUR milk into large bowl. Add pudding mixes. Beat with wire whisk 1 minute. Gently stir in whipped topping. Spread ½ the pudding mixture over crackers in pan. Place 9 of the remaining crackers over pudding; top with remaining pudding mixture and crackers.

REMOVE lid and foil from frosting. Microwave frosting in container on HIGH 1 minute. Spread evenly over crackers.

REFRIGERATE 4 hours or until set.

Makes 15 servings

Preparation Time: 20 minutes
Refrigerating Time: 4 hours

In the early 1920's, Angus McDonall created a series of JELL-O illustrations under the banner of "America's Most Famous Dessert At Home Everywhere." These depictions showed JELL-O served by a monk in mission country, eyed by a bear in the mountains, placed on a prairie lunch table, eaten on a doorstop in New England, washed up on a desert island, and carried into an igloo under northern lights.

No Bake Cappuccino Cheesecake

The flavors of coffee and cinnamon add spark to this sophisticated dessert.

1 package (11.1 ounces) JELL-O No Bake Real Cheesecake
2 tablespoons sugar
⅓ cup butter or margarine, melted
2 teaspoons MAXWELL HOUSE Instant Coffee
1½ cups cold milk
¼ teaspoon ground cinnamon

MIX crumbs, sugar and butter thoroughly with fork in 9-inch pie plate until crumbs are well moistened. Press firmly against side of pie plate first, using finger or large spoon to shape edge. Press remaining crumbs firmly onto bottom using measuring cup.

DISSOLVE coffee in milk. Beat milk mixture, filling mix and cinnamon with electric mixer on low speed until blended. Beat on medium speed 3 minutes. (Filling will be thick.) Spoon into crust.

REFRIGERATE at least 1 hour.

Makes 8 servings

Preparation Time: 15 minutes
Refrigerating Time: 1 hour

Cappuccino, an Italian coffee topped with milk foam and cinnamon, has swept the country. This flavor is built into this convenient JELL-O No Bake cheesecake dessert.

137

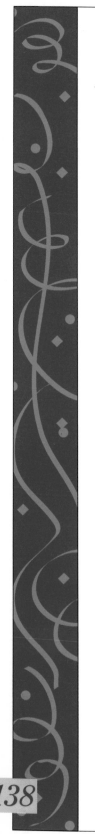

Peach Melba Dessert

A glorious fat free layered dessert.

Peach Melba was created in the late 1800's by renowned French chef Escoffier for Dame Nellie Melba, an Australian opera singer. The original version featured peach halves topped with vanilla ice cream, raspberry sauce, whipped cream and sliced almonds.

1½ cups boiling water
2 packages (4-serving size) JELL-O Brand Raspberry Flavor Sugar Free Low Calorie Gelatin Dessert or JELL-O Brand Raspberry Flavor Gelatin Dessert
1 container (8 ounces) BREYERS Vanilla Lowfat Yogurt
1 cup raspberries, divided
1 can (8 ounces) peach slices in juice, undrained
Cold water

STIR ¾ cup of the boiling water into 1 package of gelatin in large bowl at least 2 minutes until completely dissolved. Refrigerate about 1 hour or until slightly thickened (consistency of unbeaten egg whites). Stir in yogurt and ½ cup of the raspberries. Reserve remaining raspberries for garnish. Pour gelatin mixture into serving bowl. Refrigerate about 2 hours or until set but not firm (gelatin should stick to finger when touched and should mound).

MEANWHILE, drain peaches, reserving juice. Add cold water to reserved juice to make 1 cup; set aside. Stir remaining ¾ cup boiling water into remaining package of gelatin in large bowl at least 2 minutes until completely dissolved. Stir in measured juice and water. Refrigerate about 1 hour or until slightly thickened (consistency of unbeaten egg whites).

RESERVE several peach slices for garnish; chop remaining peaches. Stir chopped peaches into slightly thickened gelatin. Spoon over gelatin layer in bowl. Refrigerate 3 hours or until firm. Top with reserved peach slices and raspberries.

Makes 8 servings

 ***Nutrition Information Per Serving (using JELL-O Brand Raspberry Flavor Sugar Free Low Calorie Gelatin Dessert):*** *60 calories, 0g fat, less than 5mg cholesterol, 75mg sodium, 10g carbohydrate, 1g dietary fiber, 11g sugars, 3g protein*

Preparation Time: 20 minutes
Refrigerating Time: 6 hours

Peach Melba Dessert

Lemon Sour Cream Pound Cake with Lemon Glaze

In the early 1880's, an ad campaign proclaimed JELL-O pudding "Makes Ordinary Cake Extraordinary," pointing out that the addition of pudding makes cake moist and delicious.

A rich, velvety cake with a tart-sweet lemon topping.

CAKE

 1 package (2-layer size) yellow cake mix or cake mix with pudding in the mix
 1 package (2.9 ounces) JELL-O Lemon Flavor Cook & Serve Pudding & Pie Filling (*not Instant*)
 1 container (8 ounces) BREAKSTONE'S Sour Cream
 ⅓ cup oil
 4 eggs

GLAZE

 1 cup powdered sugar
 ¼ cup lemon juice
 2 tablespoons butter or margarine, melted
 1 teaspoon water

HEAT oven to 350°F.

PLACE cake mix, pudding mix, sour cream, oil and eggs in large bowl. Beat with electric mixer on medium speed 4 minutes. Pour into greased and floured 10-inch tube or fluted tube pan.

BAKE 55 to 60 minutes or until toothpick inserted in center comes out clean. Meanwhile, mix powdered sugar, lemon juice, butter and water until smooth.

REMOVE cake from oven. Cool 15 minutes; remove from pan. Place on wire rack. Poke cake all over with skewer. Spoon glaze over warm cake. Dust cooled cake with additional powdered sugar, if desired. *Makes 12 servings*

Preparation Time: 30 minutes
Baking Time: 1 hour

Pudding Poke Brownies

After one sampling of these luscious brownies, they'll come begging for more!

> **1 package (19.8 ounces) brownie mix**
> **1½ cups cold milk**
> **1 package (4-serving size) JELL-O Instant Pudding & Pie Filling, any flavor**

PREPARE and bake brownie mix as directed on package in an 8- or 9-inch square pan. Remove from oven. Immediately poke holes down through brownies to pan at 1-inch intervals with round handle of a wooden spoon. (Or poke holes with a plastic drinking straw, using turning motion to make large holes.)

POUR milk into large bowl. Add pudding mix. Beat with wire whisk 2 minutes. Quickly pour about ½ of the thin pudding mixture evenly over warm brownies into holes. Let remaining pudding mixture stand to thicken slightly. Spoon over top of brownies, swirling to frost brownies.

REFRIGERATE at least 1 hour or until ready to serve.   *Makes 16 servings*

Preparation Time: 15 minutes
Baking Time: 30 minutes
Refrigerating Time: 1 hour

Poke cake made with JELL-O gelatin or JELL-O pudding is one of the most frequently requested JELL-O recipes by consumers. Here's a brand new application of the "poke" technique.

Layered Chocolate Cheesecake Squares

This is the ultimate dessert for dinner guests.

> **1 package (9.2 ounces) JELL-O No Bake Chocolate Silk Pie**
> **1 package (11.1 ounces) JELL-O No Bake Real Cheesecake**
> **½ cup (1 stick) butter or margarine, melted**
> **1⅔ cups cold milk**
> **1½ cups cold milk**

MIX crumbs from both packages and butter thoroughly with fork in medium bowl until crumbs are well moistened. Press firmly onto bottom of foil-lined 13×9-inch pan.

PREPARE Chocolate Silk Pie and Cheesecake fillings separately, as directed on each package. Spread chocolate filling evenly over crust; top with cheesecake filling.

REFRIGERATE at least 1 hour. Garnish as desired.   *Makes 15 servings*

Preparation Time: 20 minutes
Refrigerating Time: 1 hour

This recipe was developed in 1984 with the introduction of JELL-O No Bake Chocolate Silk Pie.

Fruity Pound Cake

A wonderfully moist cake with just the right touch of lemon.

This recipe works with other gelatin flavors, too. Orange is excellent, or try cherry, using ½ teaspoon almond extract in place of the grated lemon or orange peel.

**1 package (4-serving size) JELL-O Brand
 Lemon Flavor Gelatin Dessert
1 teaspoon grated lemon or orange peel
1 package (2-layer size) white cake mix or
 cake mix with pudding in the mix
¾ cup water
¼ cup oil
4 eggs
 Fluffy Pudding Frosting (recipe follows)**

ADD gelatin and grated peel to cake mix.

PREPARE and bake cake mix as directed on package in two 8- or 9-inch round cake pans. Cool 15 minutes; remove from pans. Cool completely on wire racks. Fill and frost with Fluffy Pudding Frosting. Decorate as desired.

Makes 12 servings

Fluffy Pudding Frosting: Pour 1 cup cold milk into medium bowl. Add 1 package (4-serving size) JELL-O Instant Pudding & Pie Filling, any flavor, and ¼ cup powdered sugar. Beat with wire whisk 2 minutes. Gently stir in 1 tub (8 ounces) COOL WHIP Whipped Topping, thawed. Spread onto cake at once. Makes about 4 cups or enough for two 8- or 9-inch layers.

Preparation Time: 30 minutes
Baking Time: 40 minutes

Now's the time for JELL-O
SIX DELICIOUS FLAVORS

1952

Fruity Pound Cake

Pastel Swirl Dessert

A lovely dessert suitable for a shower, luncheon or any occasion!

Part of the fun of
JELL-O gelatin is
the magical way it
can be molded,
swirled, layered
and used to
suspend other
foods.

1 package (3 ounces) ladyfingers, split
1⅓ cups boiling water
2 packages (4-serving size) JELL-O Brand Gelatin Dessert, any 2 different flavors
1 cup cold water
Ice cubes
1 tub (12 ounces) COOL WHIP Whipped Topping, thawed

TRIM about 1 inch off 1 end of each ladyfinger; reserve trimmed ends. Place ladyfingers, cut ends down, around side of 9-inch springform pan.* Place trimmed ends on bottom of pan.

STIR ⅔ cup of the boiling water into each package of gelatin in separate medium bowls at least 2 minutes until completely dissolved. Mix cold water and ice cubes to make 2½ cups. Stir ½ of the ice water into each bowl until gelatin is slightly thickened. Remove any remaining ice.

GENTLY stir ½ of the whipped topping with wire whisk into each gelatin mixture until smooth. Refrigerate 20 to 30 minutes or until mixtures are very thick and will mound. Spoon mixtures alternately into prepared pan. Swirl with knife to marbleize.

REFRIGERATE 4 hours or until firm. Remove side of pan.   *Makes 16 servings*

To prepare in 13×9-inch pan, do not trim ladyfingers. Line bottom of pan with ladyfingers. Continue as directed.

Preparation Time: 30 minutes
Refrigerating Time: 4½ hours

*Celery, chocolate, coffee and apple were the least
favorite flavors of JELL-O gelatin and are therefore
no longer produced.*

145

Pastel Swirl Dessert

Chocolate Candy Bar Dessert

In 1972, JELL-O instant pudding featured "Sweet Cookie," a doll that came with her own batch of colorful, safe kitchen accessories and a recipe book filled with instant pudding desserts.

Top off a backyard barbecue or family reunion with this fabulous pan dessert.

  2 cups chocolate wafer cookie crumbs
  ½ cup sugar, divided
  ½ cup (1 stick) butter or margarine, melted
  1 package (8 ounces) PHILADELPHIA BRAND Cream Cheese, softened
  1 tub (12 ounces) COOL WHIP Whipped Topping, thawed
  1 cup chopped chocolate-covered candy bars
  3 cups cold milk
  2 packages (4-serving size) JELL-O Chocolate Flavor Instant Pudding & Pie Filling

MIX cookie crumbs, ¼ cup of the sugar and butter in 13×9-inch pan. Press firmly onto bottom of pan. Refrigerate until ready to fill.

BEAT cream cheese and remaining ¼ cup sugar in medium bowl with wire whisk until smooth. Gently stir in ½ of the whipped topping. Spread evenly over crust. Sprinkle chopped candy bars over cream cheese layer.

POUR milk into large bowl. Add pudding mixes. Beat with wire whisk 1 minute. Pour over chopped candy bar layer. Let stand 5 minutes or until thickened. Spread remaining whipped topping over pudding layer.

REFRIGERATE 2 hours or until set.   *Makes 15 servings*

Preparation Time: 25 minutes
Refrigerating Time: 2 hours

Cranberry Cream Cheese Dessert

Enjoy the tart taste of cranberries any time of year.

1½ cups boiling water
   1 package (8-serving size) or 2 packages (4-serving size) JELL-O Brand
      Cranberry Flavor Gelatin Dessert, or any red flavor
1½ cups cold water
   1 can (16 ounces) whole berry cranberry sauce
1½ cups graham cracker crumbs
   ½ cup sugar, divided
   ½ cup (1 stick) butter or margarine, melted
   1 package (8 ounces) PHILADELPHIA BRAND Cream Cheese, softened
   2 tablespoons milk
   1 tub (8 ounces) COOL WHIP Whipped Topping, thawed

STIR boiling water into gelatin in large bowl at least 2 minutes until completely dissolved. Stir in cold water and cranberry sauce. Refrigerate about 1¼ hours or until slightly thickened (consistency of unbeaten egg whites).

MEANWHILE, mix crumbs, ¼ cup of the sugar and butter in 13×9-inch pan. Press firmly onto bottom of pan. Refrigerate until ready to fill.

BEAT cream cheese, remaining ¼ cup sugar and milk in large bowl until smooth. Gently stir in 2 cups of the whipped topping. Spread evenly over crust. Spoon gelatin mixture over cream cheese layer.

REFRIGERATE 3 hours or until firm. Serve with remaining whipped topping.

Makes 15 servings

Preparation Time: 25 minutes
Refrigerating Time: 4¼ hours

A 1915 JELL-O recipe booklet cordially invited "All who receive this book before the close of the Panama Exposition at San Francisco . . . to visit the JELL-O booth there and witness the working of one of the wonderful automatic machines that puts up JELL-O."

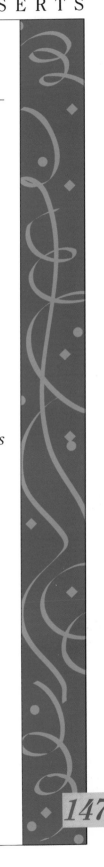

147

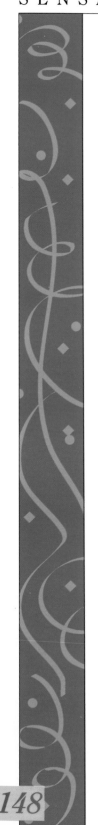

*L*emon Soufflé Cheesecake

A stunning dessert your guests will adore.

JELL-O gelatin is the largest-selling prepared dessert in America.

1 graham cracker, crushed, or 2 tablespoons graham cracker crumbs, divided
⅔ cup boiling water
1 package (4-serving size) JELL-O Brand Lemon Flavor Sugar Free Low Calorie Gelatin Dessert or JELL-O Brand Lemon Flavor Gelatin Dessert
1 cup LIGHT N' LIVELY 1% Lowfat Cottage Cheese with Calcium
1 tub (8 ounces) PHILADELPHIA BRAND LIGHT Light Cream Cheese
2 cups thawed COOL WHIP FREE or COOL WHIP LITE Whipped Topping

SPRINKLE ½ of the crumbs onto side of 8- or 9-inch springform pan or 9-inch pie plate that has been sprayed with no stick cooking spray.

STIR boiling water into gelatin in large bowl at least 2 minutes until completely dissolved. Pour into blender container. Add cheeses; cover. Blend on medium speed until smooth, scraping down sides occasionally.

POUR into large bowl. Gently stir in whipped topping. Pour into prepared pan; smooth top. Sprinkle remaining crumbs around outside edge. Refrigerate 4 hours or until set.

REMOVE side of pan just before serving. Garnish as desired.   *Makes 8 servings*

 Nutrition Information Per Serving (using JELL-O Brand Lemon Flavor Sugar Free Low Calorie Gelatin Dessert and COOL WHIP FREE and omitting garnish):
130 calories, 6g fat, 20mg cholesterol, 280mg sodium, 11g carbohydrate,
0g dietary fiber, 5g sugars, 7g protein, 10% daily value calcium

Preparation Time: 20 minutes
Refrigerating Time: 4 hours

Lemon Soufflé Cheesecake

Creamy Lemon Bars

Luscious, lemony treats—perfect with an afternoon cup of tea or glass of milk.

Lemon was one of the original flavors of Genessee Pudding Powder, a line which was acquired by the JELL-O Company in 1928.

1½ **cups graham cracker crumbs**
½ **cup sugar, divided**
½ **cup (1 stick) butter or margarine, melted**
1 **package (8 ounces) PHILADELPHIA BRAND Cream Cheese, softened**
2 **tablespoons milk**
1 **tub (8 ounces) COOL WHIP Whipped Topping, thawed**
1 **package (4.3 ounces) JELL-O Lemon Flavor Cook & Serve Pudding & Pie Filling (*not Instant*)**
¾ **cup sugar**
3 **cups water, divided**
3 **egg yolks**

MIX crumbs, ¼ cup of the sugar and butter in 13×9-inch pan. Press firmly onto bottom of pan. Refrigerate until ready to fill.

BEAT cream cheese, remaining ¼ cup sugar and milk until smooth. Gently stir in ½ of the whipped topping. Spread evenly over crust.

STIR pudding mix, ¾ cup sugar, ½ cup of the water and egg yolks in medium saucepan. Stir in remaining 2½ cups water. Stirring constantly, cook on medium heat until mixture comes to full boil. Cool 5 minutes, stirring twice. Pour over cream cheese layer.

REFRIGERATE 4 hours or until set. Just before serving, spread remaining whipped topping over pudding. *Makes 15 servings*

Preparation Time: 25 minutes
Refrigerating Time: 4 hours

Pistachio Pudding Cake

Serve this to the leprechauns on St. Patrick's Day . . . and other days, too.

1 package (2-layer size) yellow cake mix*
1 package (4-serving size) JELL-O Pistachio Flavor Instant Pudding & Pie Filling
4 eggs
1¼ cups water*
¼ cup oil
½ teaspoon almond extract
7 drops green food coloring (optional)
Powdered sugar

The range of colors and flavors available with JELL-O products makes them suitable for any special occasion, complementing any party concept or color scheme.

HEAT oven to 350°F.

PLACE all ingredients except powdered sugar in large bowl. Beat with electric mixer on low speed just to moisten. Beat on medium speed 4 minutes. Pour into greased and floured 10-inch fluted tube or tube pan.

BAKE 50 to 55 minutes or until toothpick inserted in center comes out clean.

REMOVE cake from oven. Cool 15 minutes; remove from pan. Cool completely on wire rack. Dust with powdered sugar just before serving. *Makes 12 servings*

*Or use cake mix with pudding in the mix and reduce water to 1 cup.

Preparation Time: 20 minutes
Baking Time: 55 minutes

JELL-O® *Fun Facts*

In 1913, Rosie O'Neill, creator of the famous rosy-cheeked Kewpie Dolls, illustrated a full-color Kewpie Doll JELL-O Book, showing the little imps making and garnishing a variety of beautiful salads and desserts.

151

Tropical Terrine

Canned pineapple has always been a favorite ingredient in JELL-O gelatin recipes.

Refreshing island flavors for any time of year.

1 package (3 ounces) ladyfingers, split
1½ cups boiling water
1 package (8-serving size) or 2 packages
    (4-serving size) JELL-O Brand Island
    Pineapple Flavor Gelatin Dessert
1 can (8 ounces) crushed pineapple in juice,
    undrained
1 cup cold water
2 cups thawed COOL WHIP Whipped Topping
1 can (11 ounces) mandarin orange
    segments, drained

LINE bottom and sides of 9×5-inch loaf pan with plastic wrap. Stand enough ladyfingers to fit evenly along sides of pan (cut sides should be facing in).

STIR boiling water into gelatin in large bowl at least 2 minutes until completely dissolved. Stir in pineapple with juice and water. Refrigerate about 1¼ hours or until slightly thickened (consistency of unbeaten egg whites). Gently stir in whipped topping and oranges. Spoon into prepared pan. Arrange remaining ladyfingers evenly on top of gelatin mixture.

REFRIGERATE 3 hours or until firm. Unmold. Garnish as desired.   *Makes 12 servings*

Preparation Time: 30 minutes
Refrigerating Time: 4¼ hours

Now's the time for JELL-O
SIX DELICIOUS FLAVORS

When a bunch of youngsters get together, there's bound to be some gay goings-on! And there's bound to be some big dishes of Jell-O ready and waiting for them to dig into—if there's a wise "mom" in the house! Jell-O gelatin desserts always cost so little . . . and always please so much!

1952

Tropical Terrine

Pudding Poke Cake

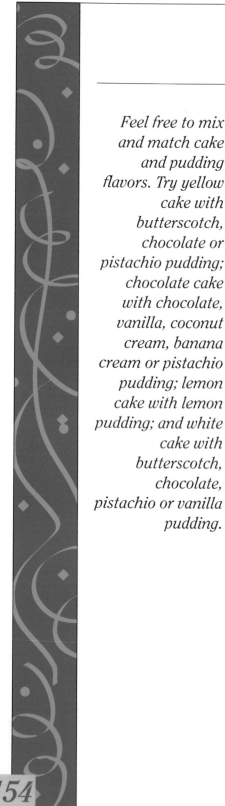

Feel free to mix and match cake and pudding flavors. Try yellow cake with butterscotch, chocolate or pistachio pudding; chocolate cake with chocolate, vanilla, coconut cream, banana cream or pistachio pudding; lemon cake with lemon pudding; and white cake with butterscotch, chocolate, pistachio or vanilla pudding.

A favorite with everyone . . . and so easy to make.

> **1 package (2-layer size) chocolate cake mix or cake mix with pudding in the mix**
> **4 cups cold milk**
> **2 packages (4-serving size) JELL-O Vanilla Flavor Instant Pudding & Pie Filling**

PREPARE and bake cake mix as directed on package for 13×9-inch baking pan. Remove from oven. Immediately poke holes down through cake to pan at 1-inch intervals with round handle of a wooden spoon. (Or poke holes with a plastic drinking straw, using turning motion to make large holes.)

POUR milk into large bowl. Add pudding mixes. Beat with wire whisk 2 minutes. Quickly pour about ½ of the thin pudding mixture evenly over warm cake and into holes. Let remaining pudding mixture stand to thicken slightly. Spoon over top of cake, swirling to frost cake.

REFRIGERATE at least 1 hour or until ready to serve. *Makes 15 servings*

Preparation Time: 30 minutes
Baking Time: 40 minutes
Refrigerating Time: 1 hour

The five most requested JELL-O recipes are Gelatin Poke Cake, COOL 'N EASY® Pie, Pudding Poke Cake, JIGGLERS® and Fruity Gelatin Pops.

*L*emon Berry Terrine

A spectacular creation, with whole berries and creamy filling inside a cake "box."

> 1 package (12 ounces) pound cake
> 1 package (8 ounces) PHILADELPHIA BRAND Cream Cheese, softened
> 1½ cups cold milk, divided
> 1 package (4-serving size) JELL-O Lemon Flavor Instant Pudding & Pie Filling
> 1 teaspoon grated lemon peel
> 1 tub (8 ounces) COOL WHIP Whipped Topping, thawed
> 1 pint strawberries, hulled, divided

LINE bottom and sides of 8×4-inch loaf pan with waxed paper.

CUT rounded top off cake and trim edges of cake; reserve for another use. Cut cake horizontally into 5 slices. Line bottom and long sides of pan with 3 cake slices. Cut another cake slice in half; place on short sides of pan.

BEAT cream cheese and ½ cup of the milk in large bowl with electric mixer on low speed until smooth. Add remaining milk, pudding mix and lemon peel; beat 2 minutes. Gently stir in 1 cup of the whipped topping.

SPOON ½ of the filling into cake-lined pan. Arrange ½ of the strawberries, stem-side up, in filling, pressing down slightly. Top with remaining filling. Place remaining cake slice on top of filling.

REFRIGERATE 3 hours or until firm. Invert pan onto serving plate; remove waxed paper. Garnish with remaining whipped topping and strawberries.

Makes 16 servings

Preparation Time: 30 minutes
Refrigerating Time: 3 hours

Special JELL-O desserts have always been favorites for entertaining. This one is surprisingly easy, but delivers a dramatic impact.

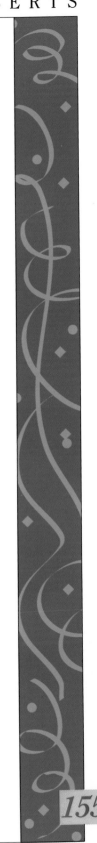

155

Berried Delight

A new berry season sensation.

1½ **cups graham cracker crumbs**
½ **cup sugar, divided**
½ **cup (1 stick) butter or margarine, melted**
1 **package (8 ounces) PHILADELPHIA BRAND Cream Cheese, softened**
2 **tablespoons milk**
1 **tub (8 ounces) COOL WHIP Whipped Topping, thawed**
2 **pints strawberries, hulled, halved**
3½ **cups cold milk**
2 **packages (4-serving size) JELL-O Vanilla Flavor Instant Pudding & Pie Filling**

MIX crumbs, ¼ cup of the sugar and butter in 13×9-inch pan. Press firmly onto bottom of pan. Refrigerate until ready to fill.

BEAT cream cheese, remaining ¼ cup sugar and 2 tablespoons milk until smooth. Gently stir in ½ of the whipped topping. Spread over crust. Top with strawberry halves.

POUR 3½ cups milk into large bowl. Add pudding mixes. Beat with wire whisk 2 minutes. Pour over cream cheese layer.

REFRIGERATE 4 hours or until set. Just before serving, spread remaining whipped topping over pudding.   *Makes 15 servings*

Preparation Time: 30 minutes
Refrigerating Time: 4 hours

Berried Delight

Holiday Specialties

Holidays coming up? A beach-y July 4th, crisp Thanksgiving or merry Yuletide? Getting ready for them is fun, but a real challenge, too, because there never seems to be enough time.

The colors, flavors and textures of JELL-O brand gelatins and puddings are perfect for special happenings. And that's what this chapter is all about. More importantly, most recipes here take 20 minutes or less to prepare before they are refrigerated.

So, brighten a holiday gathering with a Luscious Lemon Poke Cake, dazzle them at a July 4th barbecue with a spectacular "Red, White and Blue" Mold, spook the scarecrows with Graveyard Pudding Dessert, or treat the turkey to a Spiced Cranberry Orange Mold or Double Layer Pumpkin Pie! Your guests will be impressed—the family will, too!

159

Top to bottom: Spiced Cranberry Orange Mold (page 162), Layered Cranberry Cheesecake (page 174), Holiday Poke Cake (page 168), Praline Pumpkin Pie (page 163)

Cranberry Fruit Mold

A 1915 JELL-O recipe book, featuring six of America's most famous cooks, had this to say: "When fruit and JELL-O are served in combination, dessert time becomes the most enjoyable part of the meal."

Three little kittens took off their mittens
Enchanted, delighted and merry.
For each was to savor a new Jell-O flavor—
Black Raspberry, Grape and Black Cherry.

JELL-O
New!
IMITATION
BLACK CHERRY FLAVOR

1956

Experience delicious fruit-filled effervescence in this delightful mold!

2 cups boiling water
1 package (8-serving size) or 2 packages (4-serving size) JELL-O Brand Cranberry Flavor Gelatin Dessert or JELL-O Brand Cranberry Flavor Sugar Free Low Calorie Gelatin Dessert
1½ cups cold ginger ale, lemon-lime carbonated beverage, seltzer or water
2 cups halved green and/or red seedless grapes
1 can (11 ounces) mandarin orange segments, drained

STIR boiling water into gelatin in large bowl at least 2 minutes until completely dissolved. Stir in cold ginger ale. Refrigerate about 1½ hours or until thickened (spoon drawn through leaves definite impression). Stir in fruit. Spoon into 6-cup mold.

REFRIGERATE 4 hours or until firm. Unmold. Garnish as desired.   *Makes 10 servings*

 Nutrition Information Per Serving (using JELL-O Brand Cranberry Flavor Sugar Free Low Calorie Gelatin Dessert and seltzer and omitting garnish): *45 calories, 0g fat, 0mg cholesterol, 65mg sodium, 10g carbohydrate, less than 1g dietary fiber, 8g sugars, 2g protein, 20% daily vitamin C*

Preparation Time: 15 minutes
Refrigerating Time: 5½ hours

161

Cranberry Fruit Mold

Spiced Cranberry Orange Mold

No holiday dinner should be without this!

Since its earliest days, JELL-O gelatin has been used as a "table jelly" to accompany meat and poultry. It is still prized for its delicious flavor and "delightful cooling quality."

1½ cups boiling water
1 package (8-serving size) or 2 packages (4-serving size) JELL-O Brand Cranberry Flavor Gelatin, or any red flavor
1 can (16 ounces) whole berry cranberry sauce
1 cup cold water
1 tablespoon lemon juice
¼ teaspoon ground cinnamon
⅛ teaspoon ground cloves
1 orange, sectioned, diced
½ cup chopped walnuts

STIR boiling water into gelatin in large bowl at least 2 minutes until completely dissolved. Stir in cranberry sauce, cold water, lemon juice, cinnamon and cloves. Refrigerate about 1½ hours or until thickened (spoon drawn through leaves definite impression).

STIR in orange and walnuts. Spoon into 5-cup mold.

REFRIGERATE 4 hours or until firm. Unmold. Garnish as desired.

Makes 10 servings

Preparation Time: 20 minutes
Refrigerating Time: 5½ hours

Praline Pumpkin Pie

The praline layer adds fabulous taste and texture to this Thanksgiving pie.

½ **cup chopped pecans or walnuts**
⅓ **cup butter or margarine**
⅓ **cup firmly packed brown sugar**
1 **prepared graham cracker crumb crust (6 ounces)**
1 **cup cold milk**
1 **can (16 ounces) pumpkin**
2 **packages (4-serving size) JELL-O Vanilla Flavor Instant Pudding & Pie Filling**
1¼ **teaspoons pumpkin pie spice**
1½ **cups thawed COOL WHIP Whipped Topping**

Traditional pumpkin pies bake for nearly an hour. This one takes only about 20 minutes to prepare and requires no baking at all!

BRING nuts, butter and sugar to boil in small saucepan on medium heat; boil 30 seconds. Spread onto bottom of crust. Cool.

POUR milk into large bowl. Add pumpkin, pudding mixes and spice. Beat with wire whisk until well mixed. (Mixture will be thick.) Immediately stir in whipped topping. Spread over nut layer.

REFRIGERATE 4 hours or until set. Garnish as desired.   *Makes 8 servings*

Preparation Time: 20 minutes
Refrigerating Time: 4 hours

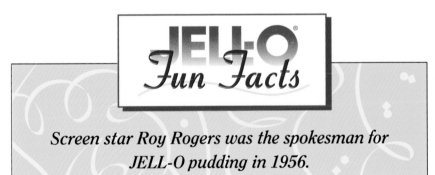

JELL-O®
Fun Facts

Screen star Roy Rogers was the spokesman for JELL-O pudding in 1956.

Double Layer Pumpkin Pie

JELL-O pudding pumpkin pies date back to the 1960's. This 1991 recipe, featuring a scrumptious double layer, requires no baking whatsoever.

Rub-a-dub-dub, three men in a tub...
Just look at the smiles on their faces!
Though lost far from shore, they've got Jell-O galore!
Now, wouldn't you like to trade places?

1955

A noble ending to the Thanksgiving feast.

4 ounces PHILADELPHIA BRAND Cream Cheese, softened
1 tablespoon milk or half-and-half
1 tablespoon sugar
1½ cups thawed COOL WHIP Whipped Topping
1 prepared graham cracker crumb crust (6 ounces)
1 cup cold milk or half-and-half
1 can (16 ounces) pumpkin
2 packages (4-serving size) JELL-O Vanilla Flavor Instant Pudding & Pie Filling
1 teaspoon ground cinnamon
½ teaspoon ground ginger
¼ teaspoon ground cloves

MIX cream cheese, 1 tablespoon milk and sugar in large bowl with wire whisk until smooth. Gently stir in whipped topping. Spread onto bottom of crust.

POUR 1 cup milk into large bowl. Add pumpkin, pudding mixes and spices. Beat with wire whisk until well mixed. (Mixture will be thick.) Spread over cream cheese layer.

REFRIGERATE 4 hours or until set.

Makes 8 servings

Double Layer Pecan Pumpkin Pie: Stir ¼ cup toasted chopped pecans into cream cheese mixture. Spread onto bottom of crust. Continue as directed.

Preparation Time: 15 minutes
Refrigerating Time: 4 hours

Double Layer Pumpkin Pie

Graveyard Pudding Dessert

Even the ghosts will go for this!

An improved JELL-O instant pudding came upon the scene in 1969—a pudding so smooth and creamy that it was deemed suitable for pie filling, too. Its name was then changed to JELL-O Instant Pudding & Pie Filling.

3½ **cups cold milk**
2 **packages (4-serving size) JELL-O Chocolate Flavor Instant Pudding & Pie Filling**
1 **tub (12 ounces) COOL WHIP Whipped Topping, thawed**
1 **package (16 ounces) chocolate sandwich cookies, crushed**
   Decorations: assorted rectangular-shaped sandwich cookies, decorator icings, candy corn and pumpkins

POUR milk into large bowl. Add pudding mixes. Beat with wire whisk or electric mixer on lowest speed 2 minutes or until blended. Gently stir in whipped topping and ½ of the crushed cookies. Spoon into 13×9-inch dish. Sprinkle with remaining crushed cookies.

REFRIGERATE 1 hour or until ready to serve. Decorate rectangular-shaped sandwich cookies with icings to make "tombstones." Stand tombstones on top of dessert with candies to resemble a graveyard.   *Makes 15 servings*

Preparation Time: 15 minutes
Refrigerating Time: 1 hour

Raspberry Giftbox

Add drama to your next meal with this surprisingly easy-to-fix dessert.

2 **cups boiling water**
1 **package (8-serving size) or 2 packages (4-serving size) JELL-O Brand Raspberry Flavor Gelatin Dessert, or any red flavor**
1 **pint (2 cups) vanilla ice cream, softened**
1 **tub (8 ounces) COOL WHIP Whipped Topping, thawed**
   Chewy fruit snack roll

STIR boiling water into gelatin in large bowl at least 2 minutes until completely dissolved. Stir in ice cream until melted and smooth. Gently stir in whipped topping with wire whisk. Pour into 9×5-inch loaf pan.

REFRIGERATE 4 hours or overnight until firm. Unmold. Decorate with chewy fruit snack roll to resemble ribbon.   *Makes 12 servings*

Preparation Time: 15 minutes
Refrigerating Time: 4 hours

Graveyard Pudding Dessert

Holiday Poke Cake

This all-time favorite is appropriately red and green for the Yuletide festivities.

2 baked 8- or 9-inch round white cake layers, cooled completely
2 cups boiling water
1 package (4-serving size) JELL-O Brand Gelatin Dessert, any red flavor
1 package (4-serving size) JELL-O Brand Lime Flavor Gelatin Dessert
1 tub (8 or 12 ounces) COOL WHIP Whipped Topping, thawed

This all-time favorite is appropriately red and green for the Yuletide festivities.

PLACE cake layers, top sides up, in 2 clean 8- or 9-inch round cake pans. Pierce cake with large fork at ½-inch intervals.

STIR 1 cup of the boiling water into each flavor of gelatin in separate bowls at least 2 minutes until completely dissolved. Carefully pour red gelatin over 1 cake layer and lime gelatin over second cake layer. Refrigerate 3 hours.

DIP 1 cake pan in warm water 10 seconds; unmold onto serving plate. Spread with about 1 cup of the whipped topping. Unmold second cake layer; carefully place on first cake layer. Frost top and side of cake with remaining whipped topping.

REFRIGERATE at least 1 hour or until ready to serve. Decorate as desired.

Makes 12 servings

Preparation Time: 30 minutes
Refrigerating Time: 4 hours

Cranberry Apple Pie

Chopped apple and walnuts add delightful crunch to this irresistible pie suitable for any holiday gathering.

2 cups boiling water
1 package (8-serving size) or 2 packages (4-serving size) JELL-O Brand
Cranberry Flavor Gelatin Dessert, or any red flavor
½ cup cold water
½ teaspoon ground cinnamon
⅛ teaspoon ground cloves
4 ounces PHILADELPHIA BRAND Cream Cheese, softened
¼ cup sugar
½ cup thawed COOL WHIP Whipped Topping
1 prepared graham cracker crumb crust (6 ounces)
1 medium apple, chopped
½ cup chopped walnuts

STIR boiling water into gelatin in large bowl at least 2 minutes until completely dissolved. Stir in cold water and spices. Refrigerate about 1½ hours or until thickened (spoon drawn through leaves definite impression).

MEANWHILE, mix cream cheese and sugar in medium bowl with wire whisk until smooth. Gently stir in whipped topping. Spread onto bottom of crust. Refrigerate.

STIR apples and walnuts into thickened gelatin. Refrigerate 10 to 15 minutes or until mixture is very thick and will mound. Spoon over cream cheese layer.

REFRIGERATE 4 hours or until firm.   *Makes 8 servings*

Preparation Time: 20 minutes
Refrigerating Time: 5¾ hours

Although JELL-O gelatin had been used for decades in holiday cranberry molds, cranberry flavor JELL-O didn't make its debut until 1994.

169

Luscious Lemon Poke Cake

Poke Cake first appeared in 1969. A huge hit with kids, it is one of the most requested JELL-O recipes. Here, white cake is a perfect foil for JELL-O gelatin's lively colors and flavors.

1960

This refreshingly moist cake has a surprise for all inside!

2 baked 8- or 9-inch round white cake layers, cooled completely
2 cups boiling water
1 package (8-serving size) or 2 packages (4-serving size) JELL-O Brand Lemon Flavor Gelatin Dessert
1 tub (8 or 12 ounces) COOL WHIP Whipped Topping, thawed

PLACE cake layers, top sides up, in 2 clean 8- or 9-inch round cake pans. Pierce cake with large fork at ½-inch intervals.

STIR boiling water into gelatin in medium bowl at least 2 minutes until completely dissolved. Carefully pour 1 cup of the gelatin over 1 cake layer. Pour remaining gelatin over second cake layer. Refrigerate 3 hours.

DIP 1 cake pan in warm water 10 seconds; unmold onto serving plate. Spread with about 1 cup of the whipped topping. Unmold second cake layer; carefully place on first cake layer. Frost top and side of cake with remaining whipped topping.

REFRIGERATE at least 1 hour or until ready to serve. Decorate as desired.   *Makes 12 servings*

Preparation Time: 30 minutes
Refrigerating Time: 4 hours

Luscious Lemon Poke Cake

Quick-and-Easy Holiday Trifle

A festive trifle that takes but a trifling twenty minutes to make.

3 cups cold milk
2 packages (4-serving size) JELL-O Vanilla Flavor Instant Pudding & Pie Filling
1 tub (8 ounces) COOL WHIP Whipped Topping, thawed
1 package (12 ounces) pound cake, cut into ½-inch cubes
¼ cup orange juice
2 cups sliced strawberries

In the early 1950's, JELL-O puddings and pie fillings were known as "Red Letter Desserts," designed to make any day a Red Letter Day.

POUR milk into large bowl. Add pudding mixes. Beat with wire whisk 1 minute. Gently stir in 2 cups of the whipped topping.

ARRANGE ½ of the cake cubes in 3½-quart serving bowl. Drizzle with ½ of the orange juice. Spoon ½ of the pudding mixture over cake cubes. Top with strawberries. Layer with remaining cake cubes, orange juice and pudding mixture.

REFRIGERATE until ready to serve. Top with remaining whipped topping and garnish as desired.
Makes 12 servings

Preparation Time: 20 minutes
Refrigerating Time: 1 hour

Ghoulish Punch

2 cups boiling water
1 package (8-serving size) or 2 packages (4-serving size) JELL-O Brand Lime Flavor Gelatin Dessert
2 cups cold orange juice
1 liter cold seltzer
Ice cubes
1 pint (2 cups) orange sherbet, slightly softened
1 orange, thinly sliced
1 lime, thinly sliced

JELL-O gelatin, with its wide variety of fruit flavors, makes an excellent base for easy and delicious drinks for a crowd.

STIR boiling water into gelatin in large bowl at least 2 minutes until completely dissolved. Stir in cold juice. Cool to room temperature.

JUST before serving, pour gelatin mixture into punch bowl. Add cold seltzer and ice cubes. Place scoops of sherbet and fruit slices in punch.
Makes 10 servings

Preparation Time: 15 minutes

Quick-and-Easy Holiday Trifle

Layered Cranberry Cheesecake

Cheesecake dates back to Roman Empire days and still remains one of the most popular desserts of all time.

Tangy cranberries and crunchy walnuts make this festive cheesecake extra special.

> 1 package (11.1 ounces) JELL-O No Bake Real Cheesecake
> 2 tablespoons sugar
> ⅓ cup butter or margarine, melted
> 1½ cups cold milk
> ½ cup whole berry cranberry sauce
> ¼ cup chopped walnuts, toasted

MIX crumbs, sugar and butter thoroughly with fork in small bowl until crumbs are well moistened. Press firmly onto bottom of foil-lined 9-inch square pan.

BEAT milk and filling mix with electric mixer on low speed until well blended. Beat on medium speed 3 minutes. (Filling will be thick.) Spoon ½ of the filling over crust. Cover with cranberry sauce and walnuts. Top with remaining filling.

REFRIGERATE at least 1 hour. Garnish as desired.   *Makes 9 servings*

Preparation Time: 15 minutes
Refrigerating Time: 1 hour

JELL-O Fun Facts

Two fictional characters called Sammy, a boy, and Watson, his dog, introduced the concept of JELL-O Snacktivities in 1992. They were shown giving up fishing for an edible aquarium, spinning along on JELL-O pinwheels, and wolfing down Star Spangle Snacks on July 4th.

Rocket Pops

Hand these out to the kids and wait for the cheers!

2 cups boiling water
1 package (4-serving size) JELL-O Brand Gelatin Dessert, any red flavor
1 cup sugar, divided
2 cups cold water
 Ice cubes
16 (5-ounce) paper cups
 1 package (4-serving size) JELL-O Brand Berry Blue Flavor Gelatin Dessert
 1 tub (8 ounces) COOL WHIP Whipped Topping, thawed

STIR 1 cup of the boiling water into red gelatin and ½ cup of the sugar in medium bowl at least 2 minutes until completely dissolved. Mix 1 cup of the cold water and ice cubes to make 2 cups. Add to gelatin, stirring until ice is melted.

POUR about ¼ cup gelatin into each paper cup. Freeze 1 hour.

MEANWHILE, stir remaining 1 cup boiling water into blue gelatin and remaining ½ cup sugar in medium bowl at least 2 minutes until completely dissolved. Mix remaining 1 cup cold water and ice cubes to make 2 cups. Add to gelatin, stirring until ice is melted. Refrigerate 1 hour.

PLACE about 3 tablespoons whipped topping over red gelatin in each cup. Carefully pour about ¼ cup blue gelatin over whipped topping. Freeze 1 hour or until almost firm. Insert wooden stick into each cup for handle.

FREEZE 4 hours or overnight until firm. To remove pop from cup, place bottom of cup under warm running water for 15 seconds. Press firmly on bottom of cup to release pop. (Do not twist or pull pop stick.)   *Makes 16 pops*

Preparation Time: 25 minutes
Refrigerating Time: 1 hour
Freezing Time: 6 hours

JELL-O and kids have been fast friends from the beginning. In fact, a 1924 recipe book called "The JELL-O Girl Entertains" included this dedication: "When you write a book you ded-i-cate it. That means you sort of christen it with thoughts of someone you love. I ded-i-cate this one to all the little girls in the world. I hope they will like My Book."

Merry Cherry Holiday Dessert

An easy but spectacular finale to any holiday meal.

Speed-scratch cooking has really taken hold in the 1990's. This recipe is a fine example of achieving great results with convenience products. After all, JELL-O was one of the first convenience products available.

1½ cups boiling water
  1 package (8-serving size) or 2 packages (4-serving size) JELL-O Brand Cherry
    Flavor Gelatin Dessert, or any red flavor
1½ cups cold water
  1 can (21 ounces) cherry pie filling
  4 cups angel food cake cubes
  3 cups cold milk
  2 packages (4-serving size) JELL-O Vanilla Flavor Instant Pudding & Pie Filling
  1 tub (8 ounces) COOL WHIP Whipped Topping, thawed

STIR boiling water into gelatin in large bowl at least 2 minutes until completely dissolved. Stir in cold water and cherry pie filling. Refrigerate about 1 hour or until slightly thickened (consistency of unbeaten egg whites). Place cake cubes in 3-quart serving bowl. Spoon gelatin mixture over cake. Refrigerate about 45 minutes or until set but not firm (gelatin should stick to finger when touched and should mound).

POUR milk into large bowl. Add pudding mixes. Beat with wire whisk 1 minute. Gently stir in 2 cups of the whipped topping. Spoon over gelatin mixture in bowl.

REFRIGERATE 2 hours or until set. Top with remaining whipped topping and garnish as desired.

Makes 16 servings

Preparation Time: 20 minutes
Refrigerating Time: 3¾ hours

177

Merry Cherry Holiday Dessert

 "Red, White and Blue" Mold

First created in 1975, the "Red, White and Blue" Loaf recipe was revised in 1993 to include Berry Blue gelatin.

Dazzle the group on the Fourth of July with this festive molded salad!

2¾ cups boiling water
1 package (4-serving size) JELL-O Brand Strawberry Flavor Gelatin Dessert, or any red flavor
1 package (4-serving size) JELL-O Brand Berry Blue Flavor Gelatin Dessert
1 cup cold water
1½ cups sliced strawberries
1 package (4-serving size) JELL-O Brand Lemon Flavor Gelatin Dessert
1 pint (2 cups) vanilla ice cream, softened
1½ cups blueberries

STIR 1 cup of the boiling water into each of the red and blue gelatins in separate medium bowls at least 2 minutes until completely dissolved. Stir ½ cup of the cold water into each bowl.

PLACE bowl of red gelatin in larger bowl of ice and water. Stir until thickened, about 8 minutes. Stir in strawberries. Pour into 9×5-inch loaf pan. Refrigerate 7 minutes.

MEANWHILE, stir remaining ¾ cup boiling water into lemon gelatin in medium bowl at least 2 minutes until completely dissolved. Spoon in ice cream until melted and smooth. Spoon over red gelatin in pan. Refrigerate 7 minutes.

MEANWHILE, place bowl of blue gelatin in larger bowl of ice and water. Stir until thickened, about 7 minutes. Stir in blueberries. Spoon over lemon gelatin in pan.

REFRIGERATE 4 hours or until firm. Unmold. Garnish as desired.

Makes 12 servings

Preparing Time: 45 minutes
Refrigerating Time: 4½ hours

Strawberry is the all-time favorite flavor of JELL-O brand gelatin. It's also Bill Cosby's favorite.

179

"Red, White and Blue" Mold

All-American Trifle

A summer trifle perfect for any patriotic holiday.

In this ideal summer dessert, the colors and flavors of JELL-O help to dress up any warm weather occasion!

4 cups boiling water
1 package (8-serving size) or 2 packages
   (4-serving size) JELL-O Brand Gelatin Dessert, any red flavor
1 package (8-serving size) or 2 packages
   (4-serving size) JELL-O Brand Berry Blue Flavor Gelatin Dessert
2 cups cold water
4 cups cubed pound cake
2 cups sliced strawberries
1 tub (8 ounces) COOL WHIP Whipped Topping, thawed

STIR 2 cups of the boiling water into each flavor of gelatin in separate bowls at least 2 minutes until completely dissolved. Stir 1 cup cold water into each bowl. Pour into separate 13×9-inch pans. Refrigerate 3 hours until firm. Cut each pan into ½-inch cubes.

PLACE red gelatin cubes in 3½-quart bowl or trifle bowl. Layer with cake cubes, strawberries and ½ of the whipped topping. Cover with blue gelatin cubes. Garnish with remaining whipped topping.

REFRIGERATE at least 1 hour or until ready to serve.   *Makes 16 servings*

Preparation Time: 20 minutes
Refrigerating Time: 4 hours

Ambrosia Mold

Try this delightful variation on a well-loved dessert.

> 1 can (8 ounces) crushed pineapple in juice, undrained
> 2 cups boiling water
> 1 package (8-serving size) or 2 packages (4-serving size) JELL-O Brand
>   Orange Flavor Gelatin Dessert
> 1¾ cups thawed COOL WHIP Whipped Topping
> 1 can (11 ounces) mandarin orange segments, drained
> 1½ cups miniature marshmallows
> ½ cup BAKER'S ANGEL FLAKE Coconut (optional)

DRAIN pineapple, reserving juice. Add cold water to juice to make 1 cup.

STIR boiling water into gelatin in large bowl at least 2 minutes until completely dissolved. Stir in measured pineapple juice and water. Refrigerate about 1¼ hours or until slightly thickened (consistency of unbeaten egg whites).

STIR in whipped topping with wire whisk until smooth. Refrigerate 10 minutes or until mixture will mound. Stir in pineapple, oranges, marshmallows and coconut. Spoon into 6-cup mold.

REFRIGERATE 3 hours or until firm. Unmold.   *Makes 10 servings*

Preparation Time: 15 minutes
Refrigerating Time: 4½ hours

JELL-O gelatin and marshmallows have always been a popular ingredient combination. Back in 1904, JELL-O Marshmallow Dessert won a gold medal at the St. Louis Exposition.

JELL-O®
Fun Facts

The first JELL-O flavors—strawberry, raspberry, orange and lemon—are still available today and are among the most popular flavors.

No Bake Eggnog Cheesecake

JELL-O No Bake Cheesecake was introduced in 1967. A boon to cheesecake fans who are short on time, this product takes just 15 minutes to prepare and goes into the refrigerator, not the oven.

Real holiday flavor with very little effort.

> 1 package (11.1 ounces) JELL-O No Bake Real Cheesecake
> 2 tablespoons sugar
> ⅓ cup butter or margarine, melted
> 1½ cups cold eggnog

MIX crumbs, sugar and butter thoroughly with fork in 9-inch pie plate until crumbs are well moistened. Press firmly against side of pie plate first, using finger or large spoon to shape edge. Press remaining crumbs firmly onto bottom using measuring cup.

BEAT eggnog and filling mix with electric mixer on low speed until blended. Beat on medium speed 3 minutes. (Filling will be thick.) Spoon into crust.

REFRIGERATE at least 1 hour.

Makes 8 servings

Preparation Time: 15 minutes
Refrigerating Time: 1 hour

Sparkling Dessert

> 1½ cups boiling water
> 1 package (8-serving size) or 2 packages (4-serving size) JELL-O Brand Sparkling White Grape or Lemon Flavor Gelatin Dessert
> 2½ cups cold seltzer or club soda
> 1 cup sliced strawberries

STIR boiling water into gelatin in large bowl at least 2 minutes until completely dissolved. Stir in cold seltzer. Refrigerate about 1½ hours or until thickened (spoon drawn through leaves definite impression).

MEASURE 1 cup thickened gelatin into medium bowl; set aside. Stir strawberries into remaining gelatin. Spoon into champagne glasses or dessert dishes.

BEAT reserved gelatin with electric mixer on high speed until fluffy and about doubled in volume. Spoon over clear gelatin in glasses. Refrigerate 2 hours or until firm.

Makes 8 servings

Preparation Time: 15 minutes
Refrigerating Time: 3½ hours

Sparkling Desserts

Holiday Fruit and Nut Mold

Sparkling molds filled with dried and candied fruits and nuts provide an excellent contrast of flavors and textures. A 1912 recipe for Fruit Pudding called for "a small handful of seeded raisins, a few nutmeats, a dozen dates, six figs and a banana, sliced."

A simple whipped topping garnish adds the perfect touch.

2 cups boiling water
1 package (8-serving size) or 2 packages (4-serving size) JELL-O Brand Gelatin Dessert, any flavor
1¼ cups cold ginger ale or lemon-lime carbonated beverage
⅛ teaspoon ground cinnamon
⅛ teaspoon ground cloves
⅛ teaspoon ground nutmeg
½ cup chopped mixed dried fruit
⅓ cup currants or golden raisins
⅓ cup chopped candied or maraschino cherries
⅓ cup toasted chopped pecans or walnuts

STIR boiling water into gelatin in large bowl at least 2 minutes until completely dissolved. Stir in cold ginger ale and spices. Refrigerate about 1½ hours or until thickened (spoon drawn through leaves definite impression).

STIR in fruits and nuts. Spoon into 5-cup mold.

REFRIGERATE 4 hours or until firm. Unmold.   *Makes 10 servings*

Preparation Time: 20 minutes
Refrigerating Time: 5½ hours

Chocolate Toffee Layered Dessert

A chocolate lovers delight!

3 cups cold milk
2 packages (4-serving size) JELL-O Chocolate Flavor Instant
   Pudding & Pie Filling
1 tub (8 ounces) COOL WHIP Whipped Topping, thawed
1 package (12 ounces) marble pound cake, cut into ½-inch cubes
½ cup chocolate flavored syrup
4 packages (1.4 ounces each) chocolate-covered English toffee bars, chopped

POUR milk into large bowl. Add pudding mixes. Beat with wire whisk 1 minute. Gently stir in 2 cups of the whipped topping.

ARRANGE ½ of the cake cubes in 3½-quart serving bowl. Drizzle with ½ of the chocolate flavored syrup. Layer with ½ of the chopped toffee bars and ½ of the pudding mixture. Repeat layers ending with pudding mixture.

REFRIGERATE 1 hour or until ready to serve. Top with remaining whipped topping.

Makes 12 servings

Preparation Time: 20 minutes
Refrigerating Time: 1 hour

JELL-O instant pudding made its debut in the early 1950's, when women were entering the work force in ever increasing numbers. Ads used the theme "Busy Day" desserts and the tagline, "Now it's Never Too Late for Real Homemade Desserts," a concept just as relevant today.

185

Index

METRIC CONVERSION CHART

VOLUME MEASUREMENTS (dry)

1/8 teaspoon = 0.5 mL
1/4 teaspoon = 1 mL
1/2 teaspoon = 2 mL
3/4 teaspoon = 4 mL
1 teaspoon = 5 mL
1 tablespoon = 15 mL
2 tablespoons = 30 mL
1/4 cup = 60 mL
1/3 cup = 75 mL
1/2 cup = 125 mL
2/3 cup = 150 mL
3/4 cup = 175 mL
1 cup = 250 mL
2 cups = 1 pint = 500 mL
3 cups = 750 mL
4 cups = 1 quart = 1 L

VOLUME MEASUREMENTS (fluid)

1 fluid ounce (2 tablespoons) = 30 mL
4 fluid ounces (1/2 cup) = 125 mL
8 fluid ounces (1 cup) = 250 mL
12 fluid ounces (1 1/2 cups) = 375 mL
16 fluid ounces (2 cups) = 500 mL

WEIGHTS (mass)

1/2 ounce = 15 g
1 ounce = 30 g
3 ounces = 90 g
4 ounces = 120 g
8 ounces = 225 g
10 ounces = 285 g
12 ounces = 360 g
16 ounces = 1 pound = 450 g

DIMENSIONS

1/16 inch = 2 mm
1/8 inch = 3 mm
1/4 inch = 6 mm
1/2 inch = 1.5 cm
3/4 inch = 2 cm
1 inch = 2.5 cm

OVEN TEMPERATURES

250°F = 120°C
275°F = 140°C
300°F = 150°C
325°F = 160°C
350°F = 180°C
375°F = 190°C
400°F = 200°C
425°F = 220°C
450°F = 230°C

BAKING PAN SIZES

Utensil	Size in Inches/Quarts	Metric Volume	Size in Centimeters
Baking or Cake Pan (square or rectangular)	8 × 8 × 2	2 L	20 × 20 × 5
	9 × 9 × 2	2.5 L	22 × 22 × 5
	12 × 8 × 2	3 L	30 × 20 × 5
	13 × 9 × 2	3.5 L	33 × 23 × 5
Loaf Pan	8 × 4 × 3	1.5 L	20 × 10 × 7
	9 × 5 × 3	2 L	23 × 13 × 7
Round Layer Cake Pan	8 × 1½	1.2 L	20 × 4
	9 × 1½	1.5 L	23 × 4
Pie Plate	8 × 1¼	750 mL	20 × 3
	9 × 1¼	1 L	23 × 3
Baking Dish or Casserole	1 quart	1 L	—
	1½ quart	1.5 L	—
	2 quart	2 L	—